"If a loon could talk, we would not understand him."
–Ludwig Wittgenstein

"Elk *can* talk, and I can understand them."
—Elkheart

Applause for David Petersen

"The world to be viewed along the shaft of one of Petersen's arrows is beautifully complex, full of shadow, light and grace."

—Terry Tempest Williams

"Petersen knows the hunt at its best and deepest."

—Christopher Camuto

"*Elkheart* is a fascinating journey into the soul of a man whose passion is the American elk, whose spirit lives deep in the mountain country and whose voice resonates with the power of the wild."

—Richard Nelson

"I have never known a more passionate hunter than David Petersen."

—Ted Williams

"David Petersen loves the outdoors and can say why."

—A.B. Guthrie, Jr.

"No intelligent reader could fail to appreciate Petersen's passion and intelligence."

—Steve Bodio

"Petersen writes with wit, clarity and transparent grace, out of expert and personal knowledge of his subject."

—Edward Abbey

"Not since Edward Abbey has someone written about the western outdoors so sweetly and with such intimacy."

—*The Los Angeles Times*

Also by David Petersen

Racks
A Natural History of Antlers and the Animals That Wear Them

Ghost Grizzlies
Does the Great Bear Still Haunt Colorado?

A Man Made of Elk
Stories, Advice, and Campfire Philosophy from a Lifetime
of Traditional Bowhunting

On the Wild Edge
In Search of a Natural Life

Cedar Mesa
A Place Where Spirits Dwell

Heartsblood
Hunting, Spirituality, and Wildness in America

Elkheart
A Personal Tribute to Wapiti and Their World

The Nearby Faraway
A Personal Journey through the Heart of the West

Among the Aspen
Life in an Aspen Grove

Among the Elk
Wilderness Images

www.davidpetersenbooks.com

GOING TRAD

OUT THERE, WITH ELKHEART

TRADITIONAL BOWHUNTING
ADVICE AND ADVENTURES, FROM
THE HEART OF ELK COUNTRY

BY DAVID PETERSEN

COVER ART AND DESIGN BY SCOTT MARKEL

Raven's Eye Press
Durango, Colorado
www.ravenseyepress.com

Petersen, David.
   Going Trad: Out There, with Elkheart. Traditional Bowhunting Advice and Adventures from the Heart of Elk Country/David Petersen
   p. cm.

1. Elk hunting
2. Traditional bowhunting
3. Ethics
4. Conservation
I. Title

ISBN   978-0-9840056-4-2
LCCN   2013937130

Cover art and design by Scott Markel
Interior design by Lindsay J. Nyquist, elle jay design
All photos by David Petersen unless otherwise noted.

Printed in the United States of America
1 3 5 7 9 10 8 6 4 2

Find out more about David Petersen at
www.davidpetersenbooks.com.

... for Alex Bugnon, Renaissance Man

Contents

Last winter's meat (Alex Bugnon)

Introduction

Looking a few books back, in *A Man Made of Elk*, I offered traditional archers and other seekers of elk and adventure a high-graded collection of hunting stories, advice and "campfire philosophy" (serious reflections on the hardest questions surrounding hunting), most of which pieces were written originally for *Traditional Bowhunter* magazine. But magazines can provide authors only with limited space. Consequently, stories almost always get "written short" to fit the magazine space available. Columns, in particular – like my long-running TBM column "Campfire Philosopher," co-authored with Dr. Dave Sigurslid – are written to a predetermined (generally one-page) length and not a word more. Thus, a distinct advantage for readers as well as for writers of collecting former magazine pieces into a book is that it provides a welcome opportunity to work back through, stretching out and fleshing out the stories in order to restore any significant missing bits. And also to correct any errors and address any arguments or other issues from readers of the original version.

That's precisely what I've done here in *Going Trad*, in the process, I hope, adding a degree of freshness and at times even a bit of spirited "outrageousness" to the material. Additionally, a careful search of my oldest, pre-TBM article files exhumed a few resilient pieces written originally so long ago, for a variety of publications, as to be all but forgotten, at least by their author. The few best of those, likewise, have received updates, additions, corrections and other makeovers and are included here. Finally, a few chapters here are spankin' new, having never before seen print.

So to that degree, *Going Trad* could be considered a sequel to *A Man Made of Elk*. Yet there's one significant difference: In the months-long process of compiling and editing material intended for this book – stories, advice and campfire philosophies, just as in *A Man Made of Elk* – I realized I had too much for a single book. Additionally, the amount of what I considered good campfire philosophy material more than equaled the other two categories (hunting stories and how-to) lumped together. Consequently, I decided to collect the campfire philosophy pieces in one book – titled *The Good Hunt* and forthcoming soon enough – and the "Me and Joe Went Huntin'" stories and how-to advice in the book you're holding now (and thank you for that, by the way). While most of what follows has to do with elk and elk hunting, I've included a couple of whitetail adventures and my best advice on hunting bear and turkey ... for comic relief if nothing else.

Very well, then: Let's get out there and go huntin!

Acknowledgments

I'm deeply grateful to Scott Markel for his attractive cover design based around "my" clever new "Elkheart" logo, also designed by Scott. I've had that nickname for decades, originally coined by my wife as half-truth, half family joke. But it's always been slightly embarrassing and consequently rarely used. Only after seeing Scott's clever logo (designed not for me but for Gregg "Java Man" Coffey's new line of Elkheart long-bows) did I feel motivated to half-seriously put the Elkheart *nom de plumb* to work. Thanks, Scott, for that spark of egotistic self-indulgence (I think).

My Arkansas whitetail-hunting amigo Joseph "Jody" Smotherman's no-BS criticisms of the work in progress comprise a generous contribution to *Going Trad*, inside and out. *Muchas gracius, Jose.*

Big thanks to Thomas Downing for allowing me to include in this collection his heart-pumping retelling of an outstandingly memorable elk hunt together. Sandwiched in the middle of three generations of accomplished trad bowhunters, Thomas sets a quietly grand example for what a vast majority of bowhunting and bowhunters must become in future if we are to survive and prosper with pride.

Ken Wright, fellow Abbey-inspired writer and publisher at Raven's Eye Press, along with book designer Lindsay Nyquist, have once again been a joy to conspire with while piecing together the crossword puzzle that is a book. To show my appreciation to all these friends and more, the next round of Patron shooters is on you!

—David Petersen
San Juan Mountains, Colorado

CHAPTER 1

The Best (Hunting) Month of My Life...
ON-believable!

When the disembodied head surfaced silently from the sea of green around me, I was so startled I almost spewed my tea.

For half an hour I'd been hunkered in the chilly morning shade in a makeshift brush blind. My longbow, loaded and ready, was propped upright against a nearby stump. Sitting there, I felt smug in the conviction that the surrounding vegetation was so dense and dry I could hear an elk coming from a hundred yards away. Consequently, I was far too relaxed and in fact had just chugged the final sip of hot tea from my thermos when my peripheral vision (always on the job, even when my conscious mind is on vacation) caught an ear-flicker of movement and I looked up and saw the big brown head, like a periscope with ears, swiveling this way and that from an ocean of aspen saplings edging a shallow pond to my front. With the breeze in my favor and me motionless in the shade, the big head detected no trouble and soon led an even bigger body out into the open and onto the soft sucking mud of the wallow. And there my surprise visitor stopped and stood, broadside at 14 yards, gazing the other way.

In a single slow motion I retrieved my bow, scooted my butt a bit sideways on the log seat of my half-assed brush blind to get into a better shooting position, and came to full draw.

Ah, but it was all just a game; practice, if you will. Even though I'll admit to a mild attack of "target envy" in the face of such a perfect set-up, I had no intention of shooting a cow this morning, just the second Saturday, day eight of the month-long Colorado elk season. In fact I had no inclination to shoot a cow anytime during the almost three weeks of season yet to come. This year I was after a bull. And not just any bull at that. Consequently, having assured myself I could make meat of the cooperative cow had this been a normal year, I let down, laid my bow across my lap and watched the rise and fall of the fall-fat animal's heavy ribs as she breathed in and out, her neck now craned around and staring back over her left rump into the aspen jungle from whence she'd recently emerged with such ghostly grace and silence.

My restraint in not killing the cow was rewarded within the minute, when I heard a second elk approaching along the same hidden trail the cow had used. And this animal, I knew from the boldly careless racket it was making, was a bull, reckless in his rutty turmoil. And this time, longbow still across my knees, I was ready.

But as soon as the bull appeared I once again relaxed. It was a perfectly symmetrical 5x5, but the antlers were small. In fact, he was a small-ish bull in every way, no larger than the cow, which, moments after the bull arrived, had turned and walked uphill into the woods, soon disappearing from sight and sound. Whether this was a well-antlered young bull or a runty older bull I could not say, though the former looked most likely. But I did know immediately that I wouldn't shoot him. And once again, my restraint was rewarded – though in a significantly different way this time – when the testosterone-drunken animal started stomping the muddy water as if he had a grudge against it, then leaned down to stab at the muck with his perfect little antlers, then flopped onto his right side, like a horse taking a dust bath, and seriously began to wallow.

For the next 20 delightful minutes the bull rocked from side to side, rolled his neck mane against the wallow bank to leave deep linear impressions, kicked his hooves in the air, ploughed and stirred the mud with his antlers, stood to shake his dripping black neck mane and urinate on his underbelly and throat, then wallowed some more. And never once was he farther from the tip of my broadhead than 15 yards. And never once did he stop to inspect his surroundings or otherwise evidence the least bit of caution. And when he finally left at a mud-slinging trot, as if belatedly realizing his one-cow harem had deserted him, the only part of his body that wasn't glistening black with oily wallow muck was a six-inch-wide stripe along his spine. "Skunk bull," I promptly dubbed him.

As you've likely determined by now, I passed on those two sure-thing wapiti that morning because I was "trophy" hunting. Nothing peculiar about that – except in my peculiar case. I hadn't hunted intentionally for horns since 1994, when I'd killed a bull whose horse-sized skull and old-growth antlers now dangerously dominate the living room of our tiny mountain cabin. (Still today, when Caroline or I accidentally whack our head into one of the long lower tines, projecting inconveniently out over the stereo, we try to laugh off the pain and utter the family joke: "Revenge of the elk!") Although that bull beats the Pope and Young minimum qualifications to pieces, the record book business holds no interest whatsoever; in fact it rather repulses me. Antlers are art and memories, not points and ego.

Across all the years since then, 1994, my trophy of choice has been meat, and still is. Of course, should it happen that a year's meat comes from a 10x10 bull, even better! But the point is that most years I kill the first healthy looking elk, of either sex, that gives me a sure-thing shot opportunity. (Most such donors, coincidentally, have happened to be middling branch-antlered bulls.) For a couple of years I even underwent a "trophy calf" stage, having become convinced that calf meat is the best meat. And yes, calves do eat good ... but they sure don't eat long and one Bambi just isn't enough to last C and me through the year. Not even close. And too, after we got some personal experience under our belts, Caroline and I decided that calf meat, like fawn flesh or veal, is a bit *too* tender and not as satisfyingly flavorful as more mature meat. (For that very reason, elk calf would make excellent "starter" meat for spouses and children and others unaccustomed to the distinct flavors and textures of game and needing a gentle break-in experience.) Since spike bulls are illegal in Colorado (part of a management plan that has excelled in producing more and bigger branch-antlered bulls), I finally settled on young adult cows and bulls as the overall best trophy meat, combining the tenderness of youth with a fuller flavor and several times the poundage of meat worn by an average calf.

So this season was an anomaly. Nor had it been planned that way. Through various experiences during opening week – first and most significantly being a huge bull traveling with 15 cows (I don't know if he was actively herding them or not), which I saw within rifle range on September 1 – the year had quickly shaped itself into something wholly unexpected and I soon found myself having both confidence and motivation enough to hold out for a really Big Boy bull. And the longer I hunted, the stronger that conviction grew.

By way of background, massive local wildfires in the bad dry summer of 2002 had utterly evaporated my beloved local old-growth forests, save for a few precious unburned bits here and there, and set the stage for a blossoming of foraging and hiding habitat so rich that fat elk, within a few years after the fires, were everywhere. Flash forward to the present hunt and I realized that in all my years of hunting Colorado wapiti I'd never before seen so many *really big bulls* as I was seeing this year, almost from day one. Nor had I ever before heard so many elk singing and chirping so tirelessly around the clock, day after night without surcease. And let's face it, even for a meat hunter, at least during the early archery season when the rut is raging, *bull* hunting *is* elk hunting. *All* of the most exciting and enticing elements of pursuing wild wapiti in wild surroundings accrue to bulls in rut. It's the bulls, after all, that create the horn-scarred aspens and excoriated conifer saplings that so excite us when we find them while scouting or hunting. And occasionally I've even gotten to hear and see those wild antler-thrashing episodes as they were playing out. Likewise, it's the bulls that make and use wallows and spread that funky ancient stench, which, though evolved to excite broody cow elk, boils the hunter's blood as well. It's the bulls that bugle, grunt, roar and scream, prompting the hunter's heart to hammer even when he can't see the singers. In sum, it's all of this and more – all this glorious bully-boy stuff – I miss the most when the early archery elk season is over. And consequently, like most, I always go afield holding out hope to bag a Big Boy, though I rarely make any special effort to do so … not at least if that effort stands between me and meat on the table.

Yet once in a while, even a meathead like me has to give in and go for the gold, just for the incomparable challenge of doing so.

All of which background led me to hold my fire at the Skunk bull wallow that entertaining morning, contentedly passing sure-kill shots at prime meat animals in hopes of getting a crack at a set of horns even bigger than the beautiful 1994 tree of a rack already on the cabin wall. Or nothing. Right to the last minute of the last day of the season: that is true trophy hunting. That was what I'd not done in decades. And this day, this season, that was my resolve. (A resolution that was made much easier to stick to, I must admit, by having a late-season cow tag in reserve. Ho-ho! The best of both worlds.)

[5]

The Skunk Bull Wallow

Elkheart's best bull, 1994

The evening of the same morning I'd watched the Skunk bull go wild in a wallow, a mile and more downhill from that wallow I spotted the same bull again – the smallish body and small but perfect antlers easily distinguished him – though now he was all spic and span again, having dried and shed off the morning's pissy mud. As I sat in evening ambush over a spring pool, the Skunk bull trotted past on an open hillside some 60 yards out. And no sooner had he come and gone, I came to understand why he'd been moving so fast, punctuated with frequent brief stops to turn and glance at his back trail, when a 6x6 came into sight, following the same invisible trail the Skunk was on. While I didn't sense that the six-by was chasing or even intentionally following the five-by, the Skunk bull clearly was trying to open some distance between. While the bigger bull was still not big enough for the mood I was in, and way too far in any event (though had I been interested, I'd certainly have tried cow-calling him into range), seeing elk, any elk at any distance, is always fun. So I just relaxed and enjoyed these latest sightings without being disappointed at their teasing nature.

And so this increasingly action-packed hunting season continued to build in promise, day after invigorating day, reaffirming my resolve to hold out for a Big Boy.

The very next day, in fact, after chasing the sound of retreating bugles and chirping cows a couple of miles uphill only to have the herd predictably outrun me and disappear from my mediocre eyes and ears, I was whiling away the midday downtime lounging in a makeshift ambush near yet another spring when three cows, two calves and a 4x4 came in to drink. Two of the cows, one of the calves and the little bull took turns drinking and watching for danger and with care and luck I could have killed any one of them. So far as elk *sightings* and passed-up shots go, this was already a banner month. And it was less than half over.

Although the bugling was nearly nonstop and some sort of elk action came daily, the first close call I had with a bull I would have loved to bring home came a couple of mornings later. The drama of the long and painstaking stalk that ensued remains a standout in my elking memory album, so please indulge me a retelling:

Just before daylight, as usual, I was on the mountain waiting for a bugler to sing so that I could give chase. While the elk music can be fantastic in the evenings as well, late-day bulls, in my experience, tend not to start sounding off consistently enough early enough to track their movements and execute a strategic stalk (as opposed to simply blundering in the bugler's general direction). And too, evening bulls in rut are almost always moving fast, filled with anticipation and energy for the night to come. Consequently, most evenings there just isn't enough time to do it right and follow through. That's why I mostly sit in ambush in evenings, hoping someone will get thirsty, saving the dramatic chase scenes for the mornings, when I have plenty of time and don't feel rushed no matter where the chase may lead.

This memorable morning, I could hear bugling from the moment I turned off my truck's engine, before I even opened the door to get out.

Whoopee! I thought, leaping out of the truck, strapping on my pack and tossing a near-full cup of java onto the ground; no time for such luxury just now.

Here we go again!

The bugler sounded to be well over half a mile distant and all of that distance, I knew, was uphill across terrain heavily littered with the fire-blackened corpses of fallen trees. On a positive note, moving uphill early always puts the cold dawn downhill thermals refreshingly in your face. Since no other bulls were sounding off between me and the distant bugler, I moved out fast, fearing that if I played tippy-toes in getting there he'd be gone before I arrived. Even so, it took me almost half an hour of hard breathing to reach the base of the thinly timbered knob from atop which the singer was belting out his ballsy blues to the accompaniment of frequent vocal eruptions from what sounded like a lot of cows and calves. My final approach, up a steep and rock-pocked slope, would be tough, if not impossible to pull off without making a racket and getting caught. Watching from a safe distance through binoculars, I could see flashes now and again as elk appeared to be running around in circles atop the knob, with maybe an acre of space up there at most. As I long ago learned the good old-fashioned hard way, when these rutty herd "raves" are happening it's pointless trying to comprehend what's going on or why. It's simply frenetic and everyone sure seems to be having fun and even with marginal wind conditions the noise and confusion provides a stellar opportunity to stalk right up on 'em.

Which is not to suggest it's easy even then. It's merely possible and I wasted no time scuttling bent-over across the semi-open brushy bottom until I was hard against the base of the knob. From there, so long as they stayed on top, my climb would be invisible. The best strategy, I figured, would be to identify a route that offered the most stable and thus quietest approach, then ease up to the rim where I could see and shoot, setting up there to wait for the bull's ongoing roundabouts to bring him 'roundabout to me. Not only the best, but the only practical option I had.

The slope, as it had appeared, was as rocky as a gravel pit, with few trees but plenty of low brush to pull myself up by and hide behind as I went. Moving only when the bull was bugling or the cows chattering (which, happily, was most of the time), taking great care not to dislodge a rock to go banging and clattering down the slope and embarrass me, and even with no more than 50 yards to the top, it nonetheless took 20 minutes to get there. As it turned out, when I finally reached a spot where I could see, and if an opportunity arose, shoot over the rim, I knelt behind a fallen log where my outline was low and at least partially screened by a small bush, knocked an arrow and gave a couple of cow chirps.

Since I could hear the bull screaming on the far side of the knob, and hear the stampeding hooves of running elk, I figured it was safe to use the call and maybe even a good idea (which most often calling at elk is not). Yet I also rather expected the minimal volume of my chirps and mews to be lost in the background noise. And I was wrong on both counts. An elk had indeed heard my calls and came straight at me in response. But of course it was a cow. And now I was pinned down as that cow stared suspiciously at my half-hidden form from a mere 15 yards, obviously seeing something she didn't like. (Or maybe, as so often happens when you call animals in close, they become alarmed by what they *don't* see, namely the alleged critter that's doing the calling.) Acting increasingly suspicious, the cow had me nailed in place if not yet pegged for what I was. Every few seconds she'd take another cautious step closer.

Meanwhile, heard but unseen in the near distance behind my nemesis cow, the remainder of the herd continued to rock 'n roll, oblivious to the little drama playing out nearby. So long as the suspicious cow didn't get close enough to smell me (not likely, since the morning breeze was still flowing downhill), and so long as I didn't even blink (well, actually I could have blinked since I was wearing sunglasses; but you know what I mean), hope remained that she would lose interest and return un-spooked to the herd. The tense standoff dragged on.

Suddenly and finally the cow turned and took off at a trot, though I had no idea how I had spooked her. Whatever; I figured I was busted and she'd alert the herd and they'd be gone and I'd be left depressingly elkless in the elk woods, as so very often before.

Then, just a moment after the fleeing cow disappeared – well, here she came back again, still running but now *toward me*. A moment later I knew why, as a Big Boy 6x6 – at first glance I guessed 350 — appeared, hot on her hooves in pursuit. This all spun out in a blur of moments as the cow braked then wheeled hard left about five yards in front of me, kicking dirt and rock shrapnel in my face. The pursuing bull, rather than following his momentary love interest through that turn, for some reason stopped just beyond arm's reach, facing me. I recall thinking at that crazy-tense moment: "I could kill him with a spear!"

So there we were, me with no spear, kneeling uncomfortably on the ground looking almost straight up at the bull, which in turn was oblivious to me while watching the run-away cow as if trying to decide if it was worth chasing her any farther. While I had an arrow on the string and my bow upright and ready to draw, my slightest movement at that juncture would have blown the game to smithereens.

You can predict the rest of the story, I'd guess: With the bull standing right over me it was not "if "but "when" he got my scent and darn-near turned himself outside-in running away. Of course my bow arm came up seemingly on its own as my right hand touched anchor and I could have taken a stupid shot at the big beige retreating butt ... but what would *that* accomplish? I didn't care to find out, and as I listened to the bull clatter down off the far side of the knob – inexplicably bugling as he went – with the herd close behind, I relaxed and suddenly realized how badly my neck and shoulders hurt from the prolonged tension. With no further hope or ado, I shook off my pack, dug out a snack, pulled on my face mask, lay back with the warming morning sun on my bearded face and thanked the gods of the hunt for the unforgettable blessing of challenge the morning had been. Better yet, I had little doubt there would be another such morning, and likely another yet, just as good or even better. That was the sort of season it was.

After all, an animal that escapes today is an animal you can hunt tomorrow.

Enter *mi amigo especial* Alex Bugnon, a celebrated jazz pianist who grew up in a French-speaking region of the Swiss Alps, was educated all over Europe, has lived and played and hunted in New York for many years now, and who'd flown out to join me for his first elk hunt ever. Happily, Alex's faith (that is: believing wholeheartedly in a wished-for outcome with no guarantee whatsoever) would not have to be tested for long.

Our first day out there, after an exciting (a spike bull almost stepped on Alex, and blue grouse were all around) yet fruitless morning spent at the Skunk bull wallow, Alex and I were sitting out the midday slump-time on an open bench scattered with unburned pines and trimmed around with brushy oak and overlooking a dry timbered drainage below. It was warm enough in the midday sun that I'd taken off my boots and socks and had succumbed to an after-lunch nap. Some while later, a creeping patch of shade overcame me and I caught a chill and was roused back to semi-wakefulness. As I sat up and looked bleary-eyed over at Alex, who was also bootless, leaning against a tree with his eyes closed, I heard a brittle snap of limb just below the lip of the rim, then more, becoming a pattern of approaching hooves. Before I had time to whisper *"Elk,"* Alex, a veteran whitetail hunter, had rocked forward onto his knees and was hissing "Don't turn around! Don't *move!*"

So there I sat, the "expert" elk hunter caught embarrassingly off guard and unprepared while my "student" calmly whispered a running report: "Two cows, 20 yards, broadside, looking at us. Wait, now they're looking behind them and here comes … a bull!" Even as he narrated, Alex smoothly inched a hand toward his bow, leaning against a nearby pine with an arrow on the string. When finally he told me I could turn around "slowly" and look, I had to wonder why, since the beautiful 5x5 had a dead-lock stare on us, and close.

Though easily within range, there would be no shots taken at any of these elk, as we had been caught off-guard and embarrassingly (for me, at least) busted. Not totally spooked but acutely nervous, the threesome

Aspen jungle, three years after the big fire (Branson Reynolds)

Close, but unshootable

soon trotted off and disappeared over a rise above the bench, headed in the general direction of the Skunk bull wallow, from whence we'd so recently come. Immediately, Alex grabbed his bow and went trotting after the animals, loping silently, if a bit comically, over the pinecones and rocks in his socks.

Of course, my friend's impressive effort was to no avail. On his return, smiling like a madman, all that my charmingly accented friend could say, over and over again, like a mantra, was "*On-believable!*"

By now, mid-month September, every day was a thousand-bugle day, and more. When Alex and I returned to the mountain each morning at or before first light, multiple bulls were bugling. When we left each night at or after dark, multiple bulls were bugling. Yet they were moving constantly and fast and not coming to evening water, leaving us to suck their exhaust fumes as we trailed them up the mountain and down each day, up and down and never quite catching up. Another problem was the green wall of wildfire-spawned aspen saplings ... not everywhere, but most everywhere the elk ever were. Several times Alex and I found ourselves within easy range of screaming bulls, yet couldn't even see them, beyond an occasional beige flash of hide or glint of ivory antler, through the opaqueness of aspens. And even if we had been able to see those bulls, there was often insufficient clearance among the bamboo-thick saplings to raise and draw even a short (54") bow like mine. But among the aspens is where the elk were, so we were in there too, having a blast and often so close to our prey we joked we could smell their breath when they bugled and forage when they farted.

By the penultimate day of Alex's too-short five-day hunt, there were an *on*-believable *five* 350-class bulls entertaining us – including, though

I couldn't prove it, the one I'd seen back on the first of the month with 15 cows, as well as the one I'd been so close to so recently on the knob – singing almost nonstop and rarely holding still. While the herd bull's antlers were slightly higher and wider than any of the four satellites' racks, all the others (as observed through binoculars at a distance) were heavier, more "massive," one big-bodied bull in particular. In fact, the only stand-out advantage we could determine among the five look-alikes was that the herd bull consistently out-sang the others in both quantity and, apparently from the cows' collective point of view, quality. Alex, the resident musician, dubbed him Pavarotti.

And so on it went – a book's worth of nearly nonstop fun and knee-shaking close calls but no arrows set free. And that included Alex – we still don't know whether to laugh or cry about it – having passed a shot at a nice 5x5 that walked by his hillside ambush one afternoon and stopped at 12 yards, slightly angling away. As an experienced whitetail ground hunter, Alex knew that he'd never get away with drawing and re-leasing on a whitey in such a situation, and so declined the gimme shot not knowing how much slower elk are to duck and run.

Too soon, Alex's stay had come down to a final morning's hunt. That same evening, he was booked to fly back to New York City and the very next day on to Atlanta for a jazz festival that night. On his long trip home Alex would jot down his still-fresh memories of that fantastic final hunt, to wit:

"Pavarotti was singing from just below a high ridge to the north that Dave calls 'the top of the mountain,' and we decided to go up after him. While Pavarotti and a couple dozen cows churned around in an open-ing between strips of timber a ways below the ridge, he was being harassed by two challenging bulls, allowing us to stalk to within about 80 yards below the herd. At that point we hit the edge of the sapling thicket we'd been stalking through, and could go no farther without exposing ourselves. That's when it started to rain, though neither of us bothered to put on rain gear as there was just too much excitement going on to notice any discomfort. So we just stood there and watched the herd bull with his cows and two of the four big satellites, running this way and that, hoping for a chance to move closer to them. Then after a while the other two satellites appeared between us and the herd, but off to the west: one about 60 yards, the other 100 yards away on a point of red rock, and closing in fast on one other, ignoring the herd. Dave said he was going after those two "Big Boys" and invited me to try a sneak on the herd bull. There was so much bugling and cow chirping and pounding of hooves; unbelievably! So up I went, and up, mostly on my knees to avoid detection, though the rain was increasing and cut visibility, which made things a little easier. At some point a long time later I realized I couldn't catch up as the herd had by then lined out for the top. When finally I gave up my stalk and looked around, I realized I'd lost my bearings and I didn't know exactly where I was, though I knew I'd gone pretty far up. The rain continued and I was really soaked by now and getting chilly and had an airplane to catch in a few hours so I started back down and soon ran into Dave, who had lost track of the two satellites after they quit bugling and now was headed uphill, looking for me. Although I'd not taken a shot all week, it was the most exciting hunt of my life, especially that final morning … *unbelievable!*"

Even days after he'd gone home, as I read Alex's note I could clearly hear in memory him uttering his favorite term of praise in that musical French accent … "*ON*-believable!" It has since become a family joke.

After Alex's departure, I returned to the hunt next morning; no time now to slack off, even for a much-craved sleep-in. At least the rain had moved along.

Continuing the pattern the elk had set for us during Alex's stay, I resumed discreetly chasing the herd – which now comprised the most best bulls I've ever seen hereabouts in the same place at the same time, before or since and likely ever again – up and down the mountain, day after day, threading and sometimes crawling through the mixed-blessing of aspen-whips, frequently getting close enough to win an exhilarating beige glimpse of a bullish singer, but still with no shot ops. Though once, well, I just have to tell you about *this* one ...

The area I traditionally hunt, being typical West Slope Rocky Mountain terrain, is defined by a river valley with a cold trout stream rushing through its bottom and mountain slopes rising abruptly on either side with deeply eroded run-off drainages cutting like an old woman's wrinkles down to the river below. And through these wrinkles the daily thermals reliably flow: downhill early and late, uphill midday. Throughout the hunt, so far, thermals and occasional storm winds had presented a nagging challenge for me and a blessing for the resident elk herd that used the corduroyed terrain as a runway. Trouble was, whether climbing or descending, I was always behind the herd with the wind behind me, all of us moving pretty much together. This day, responding to an exceptionally excited crescendo of bugling just after lunch, I found myself once again below the scattered herd as it double-timed its way uphill. For a while I'd hoped to find a way to loop around and get above them, thus downwind, in order to set up an ambush along their projected route. But as usual throughout this hunt, the excited animals were moving way too fast for any such loop-around plan to pan out.

In the end, my only option was to tuck in close behind while zig-zagging from ridge to drainage, working the thermals to avoid being scented. My optimistic hope throughout these daily races was that one of the satellite bulls would drop to the back of the pack and become susceptible to cow-calling to longbow range. To facilitate this envisioned happy ending, just in case a bull was closer than I knew, I offered an occasional cow call, like "Hey Big Guy, I'm a plump young girl feeling lonely back here all by myself; come see about me!"

And so it went: When the elk were moving through a drainage bottom, I shadowed them from an adjoining parallel ridge. When they worked up onto a ridge, I followed from down in a parallel drainage. While the wind was always at my back and the elk to my front, the vertical separation between ridge tops and drainage bottoms allowed me to dance around the wind and stay encouragingly close to the moving herd.

By now it was late in the month and the archery season was running unsettlingly low and I'd been running these old mountains for so long now, every single day in fact, that I felt like I'd grown wings. While I often got tired, I never felt deeply fatigued. (Matter of fact, back home that very night, I would proclaim to Caroline that "At this moment, thanks to these darned elk, I'm in the best physical shape I'll likely ever be in the rest of my life." And so far, as time ticks insidiously toward personal oblivion, it seems I was right.)

When the herd finally reached the dominant ridge, I presumed, based on recent experience, that rather than dropping down the far side and out of my realm, the herd would parallel along the ridge a ways – often at a trot with the bulls still vocalizing enthusiastically – only to turn after a few hundred yards and head right back down again, often as not at a flat-out run, through an adjacent set of drainages.

The elk, it seemed, saw it as a great fun game among themselves, to be repeated endlessly, though for me an exhausting game it was. There can be few rest or feeding breaks for wapiti during the peak of the rut – that is, the late-September days immediately prior to the onset of mating – what with desperately competing bulls keeping the mood so high and wild. And I felt precisely the same about it as the wapiti I was ghosting. Calling had proven useless; I'd tried but my wimpy mews readily got trampled amongst the choral cacophony of real elk talk. And wherever the herd was drinking, it sure wasn't at one of my usual ambush springs far below. So "running with the elk" was the only game in town and that was fine by me. By this point, toward the end of a relentless month of going full-out, I'd come almost to feel that I *was* an elk, thereby living up to the nickname my wife had long ago pinned to me: Elkheart.

Anyhow, that was the overall setting, situation and mood on this particularly warm and windless afternoon as the season wound down. The herd was still above me and moving farther uphill fast, quartering across a low ridge to my left. I was close behind and a bit to one side of them in the drainage below, with maybe 50 yards separating us – when I heard the low growling bugle of the least vocal and least seen of the four satellite bulls. He was trailing behind the main herd at a fair distance and I saw in this situation precisely the opportunity I'd been working and waiting for so long.

Unconcerned about the limbs I was cracking or the rocks I was rolling and other racket I was making – "It's just another elk here, honest!" – I tore roughly through the aspen whips to get a few dozen yards uphill and downwind of the growler bull to my left … then slowed down and worked up the ridge above where I hoped the bull would be waiting, now purposely making elkish noise as I went, like a hot cow responding to the satellite's muted love song. The ploy worked and the growler bugled again as I topped the lip of the ridge. He was now directly cross-breeze from me but still at about 50 yards. With great apprehension I considered the brush and sapling-choked area between the still unseen bull and me. Cover above waist height was hard to come by, as the only mature trees were fire-blackened limbless snags. Below waist height the brush appeared impenetrable.

So there we two stood, the growler and me, he on the far side of this near-miasmic up-growth of saplings and brush, all of it still fully leafed though transitioning from green to red, orange and mostly gold. It seemed an impasse until I spotted a narrow tunnel of access leading into the midst of the tangle. Chirping urgently, like a cow in estrus, I dropped to my knees and crawled into the tunnel, hoping the bull would set aside due caution and come charging in from his side to meet me in the middle. Happily, he did just that. Better yet, a few yards ahead I could see a wee opening, no more than a few yards square but big enough to fully expose the bull's vitals should he venture there. Maneuvering into a position where I would be basically at the bull's knees if he were to cooperate, I snapped off a few branches above and around me so that I could draw and shoot if I got the chance. (And once again I felt thankful for the shortness of the bow I grasped in my left hand.) Thus prepared, I turned up the calling heat.

And sure enough, my adversary responded with a series of booming, rough-edged, deep-throated screams as he bulled through the brush toward me like a tank in a frontal assault ... only to stop just short of the clearing, as rutting bulls (and spring tom turkeys) so often seem to do, their instinctive caution kicking in just when it's needed most. Although we were now no more than 15 yards apart so that I could hear his heavy breathing and smell his heady scent, thanks to higher brush on his side I could see neither hide nor horn of this bull of my dreams. Just as I would do with a gobbler in a similar situation, I quit calling, hoping the bull would grow curious, wondering if I'd left, and move forward to check it out ... and a very few steps forward was all I needed.

The breeze, if there was any, was indiscernible.

But the Big Boy didn't move but only grunted. Knowing this was the make-or-break moment, I dropped my call back into a shirt pocket, positioned my bow vertically in front of me, then reached over and broke off a small dry oak branch, making a single distinct *Snap!*

And here he came! Rather than bugling, the bull now was making weird low vocalizations best described as punctuated gurgles (some call this low-key form of rutting vocalization "glunking"). My bow was at half-draw as the huge black hooves and lower front legs came into view, pumping authoritatively through the brush ... a few, very few, more steps and the deal would be sealed and I ...

Ka-BLAMM!

As if a grenade had gone off just in front of me, I was hit in the face and upper body with a shotgun-blast of stinging shrapnel shards ... and the bull was gone.

"Now if this isn't an act of a mean-spirited god, I don't know what is," I recall thinking, almost laughing out loud in mixed surprise and relief to still be alive as my addled mind pieced together what had just happened ... and what *could* have happened. Hearing the rifle cracks of falling dead trees near and far, an aftermath of the wildfires, had long ago become a standard scare-factor when walking in the burned portions of the San Juan National Forest, hunting or not. One man had already been killed by a falling tree, and both my wife and I had "enjoyed" repeated close scares. So it was that almost immediately I knew exactly what had happened. What I still can't comprehend is the speed and force with which a charred ghost tree can fall, with little or no warning sounds. In this event it was a hulking white fir some three feet across at the base and sixty feet tall; several tons of tree that fell suddenly and silently with no wind to coax it on. When it hit the ground the ground shook beneath me and I dropped my bow and my hands instinctively flew up to protect my face from the spray of splinter shrapnel.

How easily that could have been the bitter end, for me and/or for the bull!

As it happened, the tree fell precisely across the middle of the little clearing, politely splitting the few feet between the approaching bull and me. As I gradually calmed down and pulled my act back together and worked my way around the shattered corpse of the fallen tree, I was half expecting to find the bull pinned beneath it. Happily, he was nowhere to be found and for that I rejoiced, as I want no one's help in bagging my bull, not even a playful god's.

Shaking a bit, I must admit, I worked my way out to the edge of the big roundy of saplings and brush and found a spot to sit and chill out where no second-act falling tree could reach me. For once, I could hear no bugling near or far. After half an hour I started cow calling again, though no replies were expected or forthcoming. What had almost been "my" trophy bull was no doubt long gone and still running.

Then, after a while, came a restrained half-bugle-half-grunt, and not so far away. Collecting my junk and strapping back into my pack, I returned to sneak mode and crawled into what seemed a better position and resumed calling. And calling. And after a long time I was in fact rewarded with the best, that is the closest, look at the growler bull I'd had all season: What a gorgeous monster! While his antlers were the most compact of the five bulls, what the exceptionally dark-colored rack lacked in width and height it easily made up for in mass. That was one heavy, *massive* set of antlers. And the body! This was, I speculated, a true thousand-pound bull, so rare these days as to be almost mythical. Yet, he was doubly beyond my maximum bow range and clearly still seemed spooked by the ambush attack of the crashing tree. A few moments more and Big Boy switched ends and calmly walked away. That would be the last time I ever saw him.

That night the rain returned.

Last day of the season: wind, rain and more falling trees, all the latter at a blessed distance. A perfect day for sneak hunting, though predictably unproductive since wind *or* rain of any intensity keeps game bedded, and this day brought both. But I ventured out anyhow, not believing until I got out there that after weeks of hearing multiple bulls bugling almost without pause that the music could have so abruptly just ... stopped.

But that's precisely what had happened. In a full miserable day of slogging through the wet, moving almost constantly to keep hypothermia at bay, I saw no elk and heard nothing but the rude splatter of rain on my rain-suit hood, the relentless howl of chilly wind soughing through the trees and the occasional distant pop of another dead tree succumbing to gravity.

About an hour before dark, while sneaking downhill along the edge of a bench, staying just far enough below the adjacent ridge rim to avoid being sky-lighted or fried by lightning, straining my vision into the shadowy, fog-shrouded gloom in hopes of spotting elk bedded in the wind-eddy of the timbered bottom, feeling a bit depressed that this phenomenal month of almost daily excitement and promise was finally at its end, and ending at that on a distinctly flat note, I was blessed with the high point of the low-spirited day when an almost comically miserable-looking second-year black bear, maybe 70 pounds, appeared just below me. His long dark-brown hair was so soaked it hung straight down as rainwater sheeted off. Each time lightning strobed and thunder exploded, which was every few seconds at this point, the forlorn little bear ran a few yards then stopped and stared up at the darkening sky, like "What the hell, Boss?" Then he (or she) would shake like a dog, creating a halo of water-spray that engulfed him for a moment ... and shamble on. This poor little guy never saw or otherwise detected me and I was glad for that, as he seemed stressed enough as it was. As the bear disappeared into the foggy shadows I silently saluted him in shared misery, then turned and headed home.

It had been, hands down, the best hunting month of my life. That was 2007, and no September since has even come close, though I've made meat in every one.

ON-believable!

Alex takes a break.

CHAPTER 2

Planning a Do-It-Yourself
Public Lands Hunt

As a man of modest means and immodest cravings to experience new adventures in new (to me) wild landscapes, I've always held a coal of warmth in my heart for likeminded folks of similar circumstance and yearnings who somehow find ways to get their show on the road and go get 'er done. Usually that means saving our coins, sometimes for years, while salivating with dreams that "Someday, I'll go there and do that." Magazine articles, books and the tiny minority of good hunting DVDs add to that travel fervor, to that dream of a "hunt of a lifetime." And so it is that when I see a modest tent camp pitched alongside some semi-remote public lands back road with out-of-state tags on the vehicle — with no ostentatious motor home or penthouse travel trailer or poisonous ATVs in sight; no sign of fat-cat, soft-belly shortcuts—I always smile and wish the hardy souls in that Spartan camp the best of good luck. Sometimes I even stop to say Hi, how's it going.

But before the fun can start it takes a lot of work to make it happen when we're strangers in a strange land and balancing on a slender budget. Planning and executing a successful (that is, problem-free and fun) hunt takes deep research, a sober view of expectations and (here it comes again) a resilient preference for process over product. If all of this sounds like you, here are a few pointers that always work for me.

Start planning early

The one assumption it seems fair to make going in, is that we at least know the species of game we want to hunt. But even that could change as we move through the planning steps and unexpected realities arise, both pro and con. So start planning early. Do that and the homework becomes a big part of the fun, part of the overall process, the first leg of the trip. Wait until the last minute only if you enjoy frustration and nasty surprises. By early, I mean at least a year prior to your planned blast-off to adventure.

Choose your companions carefully

I enjoy hunting alone. In fact that's how I like it (and do it) best; always have and likely always will. But neither am I blind to the value of having a good-natured and reliable friend or two to share the day's hunting yarns around the evening campfire, help with the heavy work of making and breaking camp and, if someone gets lucky, packing meat, as well as to provide a sense of mutual security in a strange land. And too, in these rich-grow-richer times when a gallon of gas costs as much as a gallon of beer, a group of hunters can cut expenses sharply by sharing gear and travel costs. But keep the group size to what can fit into a single vehicle, else you risk crowding out your own hunting opportunities.

Personally, I would never commit to a long drive and hunting camp with anyone I haven't at least shared a day-hunt and an evening of drink and talk with. *Never* accept a friend's word that a friend of his, whom you've not met, is "a really cool guy I'm sure you'll enjoy." Same goes for a drinking buddy who may be hilarious over a few beers but less than worthless "out there" where everyone must share responsibilities and sacrifice for everyone else. *Find out first.* Blind dates are for high school, not hunting camp. Get this one wrong and you're sunk before you even set sail. Another good reason to start planning early: to have time to thoroughly vet your potential companions before it's too late.

Of course, if you have basic woodsmanship skills and the confidence that knowledge and experience bring, are content with your own company night after night and can afford the travel costs on your own, never fear going it alone.

Car camp or backpack?

Road camping is easier and way more comfortable, while backpacking will get you into bigger, wilder, quieter backcountry with more game and less competition. I say, backpack if you can and while you can. There'll be plenty of time for comfort in our graves. Yet beware that it's one thing to lug a big load of gear high into the wilderness on the day you arrive, pumped with excitement and energy. "Well," we think, "I only have to suffer this hard hike once, and then I'm set for a week of hunting and camping." But lurking in the dark woodsy shadows is an insidious villain ... success. Before you decide to put in a backpack camp several miles and far above the trailhead, think seriously about your willingness and physical ability to make perhaps four trips down and back up, down and back up, down and back up, down and back up, to pack out a big bull elk, or half a dozen trips for a moose ... then yet another trip up to bring down your camp. How many trips a day will the distance, terrain and your physical condition allow you to make? How many days, thus, will it take to get meat and camp packed out? Will you be risking losing any of that hard-won God's meat to spoilage? I have on several occasions over the years found myself in some super-rich elk honey hole with bulls nearby and odds looking high ... and suddenly coming to the realization that "I don't want to kill anything here because I don't want to have to pack it out from so high up, or so far in." The time to acknowledge your limitations is during planning, not after you're there.

Yet, there are ways, and there are ways. Here's an Elkheart approach to enjoying the solitude of a backpack hunt while avoiding getting in

A roadside base camp is comfy, but it won't get you away from the crowds.

over your head when it's time to pack that horse-deer out: Forget established trails and go bushwhacking. In many if not most roadless public lands, major hiking and horse lanes are "through" trails, meaning they start at one place and end in another, miles away. Consequently you can never out-walk the potential to encounter other folks along major trails, no matter how far you go. But aside from hunters, very few backcountry visitors ever step far off-trail, and even most outfitter camps are right on trails. To turn this timidity among others to my own advantage, I've long enjoyed following an un-trailed creek drainage or a bold game trail or a linear ridge or any other obvious landmark, perhaps no more than a mile or two before finding a pleasant camping spot with water nearby in what feels like deep wilderness even though it may be as little as a mile or two from a road. Finding elk is all about avoiding other hunters. And where you can go on wheels and sitting down is where the domesticated human herds invariably congregate.

Gear

Dodging back to the often troubling topic of "surprise success," another area that inexperienced backpack elk hunters often fail to adequately plan and prepare for is discovering that sometimes the magic *does* work and there lies a 700-pound lump of hide, bone and flesh on the ground before you, rarely in the most convenient location or position and miles from camp or car. Maybe at night. Suddenly, triumph and delight turn to panic and you feel yourself exclaim, "Oh *geeze!* What the hell do I do *now*?" This too-common fix is multiplied many-fold for eastern whitetail hunters whose cultural tradition is to gut deer and haul them out whole, more often than not with a truck, tractor or ATV. And for most of these folks, after stopping by the house for a round of congratulations from family and friends and some hero photos, the norm is to keep hauling that whole deer to the butcher shop. Thus, simply as a matter of where we live and "how it's done" there, a significant percentage of experienced whitetail hunters have little or no experience in skinning and quartering an animal where it lays—and to do it alone, maybe in the dark and rain, with a deer the size of a pony? *Whoa!* And if you're hunting alone to boot, way back of beyond ... *egads!*

Alas, there's a first time for everyone. Long ago I managed it with a spike bull, my first elk, alone and miles from home or vehicle, and so can you. But not if you haven't packed the necessary gear. Not necessarily a lot of gear, but necessarily the *necessary* gear.

First, you'll need a knife that's built for work rather than as art work (though the two are not always mutually exclusive). Twice in recent years—first with a 5x5 bull elk and later with a Coues whitetail buck — this forgetful old man managed to leave his trusty belt knife in camp and had to field dress and quarter the animals with what he had on him. In the case of the bull it was a wee little 2"-blade sheath knife I carry on my armguard for backup (about the size of what are commonly called neck knives); in the case of the whitetail it was a standard Swiss Army folding knife without a locking blade. While I had sore hand muscles for days after in each case, I was able to get the jobs done — not just gutting, but skinning and quartering too.

The point here is that you don't need a big knife to take apart big animals. In fact, I believe we're much better off with more modest-sized tools. My favorite skinners all have 3.5" blades and 4" handles. The medium-sized blade allows for more maneuverability and precision in close quarters, like when removing a hind quarter of an animal with guts still in, which is how I do it, while the larger handle provides a better grip and more leverage for tougher tasks like prying apart heavy bone joints.

A bone saw is optional if you know how to use a knife to separate bone joints. Even so, a small folding saw can help speed the deconstruction of big animals like elk while performing double duty as a wood-cutter when building brush blinds. Once, I had a cow elk die on a steep burned hillside bristling with two-inch-diameter charred aspen saplings. Before I could even begin work on the elk I had to spend half an hour cutting saplings with my folding bone saw to clear a workspace around the elk. Without the saw I'd have been in deep do-do.

Likewise, I've learned to carry heavy rubber dishwashing gloves. I could care less about bloody hands and have no worries here in the Rockies about ticks, which are generally scarce. But rubber gives a far better grip than bare hands on a blood- and gore-soaked knife handle (you may have heard the clever country saying, "Slicker than deer guts on a door knob"), while preventing being stung by yellow jackets, which can be intense in the Rockies and are attracted like flies to raw meat.

But the single most important items that are most often overlooked by inexperienced backcountry elk hunters are adequate game bags. The old-fashioned cheesecloth panels I used (along with black pepper) on whitetails as a youth just don't get it for elk or moose. And plastic bags are the fastest way to sour warm raw meat. Fortunately, years ago a local outfitter friend, T. Mike Murphy, realized this problem and designed his own line of elk quarter bags and the problem was solved. Mike's bags are made from heavy sail-cloth cotton, are huge (big enough to get an entire large deer into a single bag or an entire quartered elk into two bags), have a substantial draw cord at the top and can be washed and reused for many years. I always carry two rolled up in the bottom of my hunting pack, and when guiding I insist that my hunters carry two more. As I disassemble an animal in the field I place the skinned quarters directly into these bags, cinch the tops to keep bugs and dirt out and stash them in the shade. When I'm done with the blood and guts and ready for the pack-out, which more often than not means the following morning, I drag the meat bags to a shady spot upwind of the gut pile. That way, if a bear or lion (yes, I've known lions to scavenge gut piles) should happen to cut the scent trail and follow it to the kill, the scavenger will encounter the offal first, and with luck that will be enough to occupy him through the night and he'll not find the meat. It has always worked for me (so far).

Recently, all sorts of hunting suppliers are marketing "elk quarter bags," so they're no longer rare. I strongly recommend that you buy the biggest and best-made bags you can find. With Mike's bags I can fit an entire quartered elk, bones still in, into the two bags I always carry. When I return for the pack-out with my pack frame, I'll have one or two more bags along, depending on the size of the elk, in order to redistribute the meat into roughly equal-weight packable loads. If the trip out is long, I may debone the shoulders and hams in order to reduce weight, but I generally prefer to pack out bones and all. For starters, leg bones provide more lashing points and stability for packing. And leaving the quarters in their natural "cellophane" wrappers goes a long way toward keeping the meat clean, compared to odd slabs and chunks. And finally, when you get ready to do the butchering back home (or for the butcher's sake if you hire it done) it's far easier to tell shoulder meat from ham and high cuts from low when wrapping and labeling.

Allow me to reemphasize about the game bags, because this is both acutely important to the proper care and transport of game meat, and at the same time the most often neglected element of inexperienced elk hunter preparation: Carry enough big, heavy-duty, breathable cloth game bags to hold an entire quartered elk. Never go hunting without at least two in your pack. Wastage of meat in Colorado is a felony, and nobody needs that sort of attention.

Where to?

The West is a mighty big place. Start by going online to compare game tag availability and prices region-wide for your chosen species. Every year more hunters, understandably, want to experience the West's wildlife bounty and the millions of acres of public lands that sustain that wildness. Problem is that prime wildlife habitat on public lands is being diced into smaller and tamer shreds by the sloppy knives of haphazard energy development, road building, over-grazing, clear-cut logging and ATV abuse and over-use. The inevitable upshot of this squeeze is that western states increasingly are faced with demand that exceeds supply and so are forced increasingly toward limited-draw licenses. Depending on the species and state you're interested in, you may have to play the lottery for several years before hitting the jackpot.

But while it lasts, you can still achieve instant gratification by hunting where tags remain available. Most hunting units in Colorado, to use my home state as a familiar example, still offer unlimited (you can buy them over the counter without having to enter a lottery) either-sex archery elk tags. Yeah! Sadly, most other big game tags here have succumbed to the expanding-demand vs. shrinking-supply squeeze and gone to a lottery. In other western states, meanwhile, it's just the opposite with deer and/or antelope tags still widely available while elk tags are limited. Consequently, if you're red hot to hunt out West without waiting years to acquire preference points, you're forced (and at the same time privileged) to shop around state by state, unit by unit, until you find a destination that offers unlimited tags for the species you want to hunt.

Of course, in such wide-open territory you won't be alone.

OK, but more precisely: *Where* **to?**

In these mixed-blessing days of Internet culture, all state fish-and-game departments have websites where you can buy tags and apply for

Strap on a backpack to escape the motorized mobs. (Lane Eskew)

drawing hunts online. These same sites feature hunting regulations, maps and a wealth of other information essential to planning a happy DIY hunt and camp. Colorado Parks and Wildlife even offers a free online "Elk Hunting University."

Continuing with the same example — though the procedures are similar for most other states as well — let's say you've determined to hunt elk in Colorado. But *where* in the state, precisely, will be your best bet, all things considered? Go to *wildlife.state.co.us* and poke around persistently enough, and you'll find graphic summaries of seasonal elk population concentrations overlain on a state map. Compare late-summer (September) elk concentrations against a map showing the outlines of public lands statewide to get a good picture of promising possibilities.

Perhaps you're intrigued by, say, the White River National Forest. The official map for White River, available free online, will reveal road and trail networks, campgrounds and more, while offering a general overview of major drainages and other landscape features, as well as roads and trails. For finer detail, including shaded outlines of forests and meadows, add USGS topographical maps (quadrangles) to the mix.

To make your map study come alive, learn to navigate Google Earth, another free web resource. The bounty of topographic and vegetative detail this program can provide is staggering — from potential campsites to likely bedding areas for timberline bulls and bucks. While aerial photos remain useful, Google Earth is infinitely more fun, realistic and revealing.

But before you shout *"Eureka!"* and settle on a spot, seriously consider altitude. The availability of oxygen *will* affect your physical and mental ability to hunt as hard as you might wish or need to. Higher altitudes also greatly increase the potential for weather extremes. If you'll be camping near timberline, come prepared for scorching days, frigid nights, rain, hail, tent-ripping winds, lightning and even snow. With luck, you'll not encounter any such meteorological nastiness. But failure to *prepare* for it can spoil your picnic and even prove life-threatening.

With potential destinations narrowed down to a specific parcel of public land, like a National Forest ranger district, and with enough map study and note-taking under your hat to allow you to discuss place names and topography with at least some familiarity, it's time to start working the phones. Alas, calling public lands and wildlife managers and asking them for specific hunting-related advice is a crapshoot. Agency people are just people, some are hunters and some hate hunters, some regularly get out onto the lands they oversee, while others are glued to office chairs and computers and don't know beans about the real world outdoors. I've encountered the gamut from rude, uninformed and downright annoying office monkeys, to those who are deeply informed, warmly friendly and truly happy to help. At the least, you should talk with the Forest Service or BLM biologist for the district you plan to hunt, as well as the state wildlife manager, aka game warden, for the hunting unit in question. And for the best attention and information from agency folks, call early, way early, rather than waiting close to the season when their phones will be ringing nonstop with calls from other hunters asking similar questions.

Know the competition

At the same time you're working through the logistical questions of when, where and how, you should also be studying your quarry. As a former guide for both rifle and bow hunters from a backcountry horse camp, I've met nimrods I couldn't depend on to tell an elk from a moose from a mare. To get the most from your DIY hunt, *you*, as your own guide, must know at the very least the seasonal and daily habits and habitats of your quarry. What do these animals eat during the fall hunting seasons and at what times of day? Where does that seasonally favored food grow? Where and when are they most likely drink and bed? My advice is to avoid all the boisterous videos and Outhouse Channel programs where some overweight blowhard is trying to sell you something, in favor of solid scientific information. In addition to the many excellent natural history books oriented toward hunters' needs, check state wildlife websites for research studies and overviews concerning the species you plan to hunt.

And of course, if at all possible, consult with others who've already been there and done that.

A few words on weaponry

While a detailed discussion of appropriate weaponry is beyond the scope of this overview, do please make certain your setup is equal to the animal you hope to use it on. This is not the place for hopeful optimism. No ethical hunter will go after mega-mammals the likes of elk or moose with an under-amped bow and toothpick-arrows fronted with bullet-nosed or open-on-impact broadheads. To do so places the outcome of every shot and your entire hunt and memories of that hunt forever, in the palsied hands of luck. Going under-armed also disrespects the game and the tradition of bowhunting and greatly increases your chance of heartbreak and failure. And only recently are we coming to realize that the most important element of archery weaponry isn't the bow, but the arrow. If such terms as EFOC and Tanto tip are Greek to you, I encourage you to visit www.tradbow.com (you'll need to register but it's free), then link to the Ashby Library there. It's a whole new (though in many ways ancient) and optimistic world of knowledge about arrow lethality and if I were God it would be mandatory training for all mega-game bowhunters.

Calls and calling

If you don't own an elk bugle, save your money for beer. If you do own one, leave it at home. While truly deep-wilderness bulls at times still readily respond to bugling, even then your odds of turning all that racket and excitement into a high-odds shot opportunity are low indeed. And like tom turkeys, once a bull busts you at bugling, you won't likely hear him bugle again in daylight. Running through the woods tooting a horn is the first and worst sign of an inexperienced elk hunter and a sure way to shut the real bulls up.

Cow calling can still work magic, but it's best done with two experienced hunters using a planned set-up, and best used only sparingly, and never as an ongoing serenade as we stroll through the woods.

When nothing is happening it's natural to try for force the issue by calling. I've made the same mistake too many times myself. And there are few animals more aggressive than hunting call makers and salesmen. But resist! Don't use or even carry a bugle, and use cow calls only sparingly and subtly: That's my advice, based on long experience of screwing things up out there, and I'm sticking by it.

Eschew the motorized menace

If you've not hunted western public lands within the past decade or so, you'll just have to trust me on this one: To find both good (undisturbed) hunting and good (quiet) camping, you *must* get away from the metastasizing motorized mobs. The surest way to do that, and in some tragically motor-mobbed areas the only way, is with a backpack and the "quads" God gave us. The most tragic error the Forest Service and BLM ever made was to ignore the insidious encroachment of motorized recreation onto public lands across several decades — 4X4 Jeeps and trucks, ATVs, dirt bikes and in winter, snow machines. And now it's gotten entirely out of hand and those same agencies lack the political spine to bring it under control. Colorado wildlife officials have declared the ATV menace as the leading law enforcement problem for its wardens, while a former chief of the Forest Service likewise named the ATV invasion as one of the top threats to the health of our public lands in coming years. Elk hate ATVs and know damn well what their sudden influx each fall indicates. Where DIY hunters used to be able to camp roadside and walk a half mile or so and start getting into elk, you now have to walk farther and farther every year to find uncrowded hunting and undisturbed game.

Ironically, the success rate for motorized nimrods is far lower than for boot-powered hunters, yet the sit-down hunters still don't get it. While there are many law-abiding ATV users who do get it and never leave system roads with their machines, and are really nice people who will stop and help you in a fix long before the average yuppie in a Subaru will, a sad majority of devout "motorheads," especially when playing in the political realm, are the most selfish, short-sighted, stubborn and soulless assemblage of people I've ever encountered, much after the fashion of public lands welfare ranchers.

But excuse me for going off again. The ATV blight on public lands is a touchy topic and if you ever make it out West during big game seasons you'll soon see what I mean. Therefore, my first and foremost planning tip, even though it comes last here, is to carefully research the network of legally authorized backcountry motorized trails in the area you're considering hunting (maps showing motorized trails are available from Forest Service and some BLM offices) ... then figure out how to get as far away from them as possible.

In the end, a well-planned DIY can in fact be "a hunt of a lifetime." And if your expectations aren't overblown, most in fact are. And win or lose, like potato chips, I predict you'll find that one is nowhere near enough.

CHAPTER 3

Just Scouting
(The mountains don't give a damn!)

The summer had been hot, dry and oppressive, and that first Sunday in August promised only more of the same. Although this was the tail end of the supposed thunderstorm season here in the southern Rockies, we hadn't seen a drop of rain in weeks. It had been months since I'd climbed the mountain to check on the three springs that define my favorite elk hunting area in the high San Juan Mountains of southern Colorado, and I couldn't help but wonder and even worry, what with archery season just three weeks away. Were the springs still flowing and the wapiti using them? If either answer was no, I'd have to scout farther afield and plan new strategies. I needed, and wanted, to know.

After lunch, assessing the sea-blue sky and thickening afternoon heat, I pulled on a thin, comfortable old pair of blue jeans and a sleeveless T-shirt, laced up my nylon hiking boots, slapped a cotton cap on my egg-bald head, grabbed my always-ready fanny pack, filled two water bottles — one for me, one for Otis the handsome black Lab – and away we went.

After sweating up the relentlessly steep, densely wooded slope for what seemed like forever, the terrain finally leveled, the underbrush thinned and my breathing idled down; the hard part was over. As we rested and had a drink, I noted happily that the cloudless sky of a couple of hours before had turned all cobalt and weird, and a refreshing breeze was rattling the aspens. Just a few minutes later came a distant rumble of thunder. While I welcomed the possibility of rain, I figured the storm cell would withhold its moisture as it floated over us, to dump instead on the saw-tooth wall of 14,000-foot peaks marking the Continental Divide 20 miles to the north. That had been the norm all summer. In any event, I'd climbed all the hard way up, and damned if I'd go scurrying back down for fear of getting damp before completing my scouting mission. If it came to that, a thundershower would provide blessed relief from weeks of heat. Of course, being an experienced outdoorsman, I had emergency rain gear in my belt pack. Sort of.

Rested, eager, and energized by the cooling breeze, Otis and I ambled on, coming soon enough to a familiar ridge, just below which lay a secluded aspen bench – shady, cool, fecund, and inviting. Down the hill we went, following a deep-worn and dusty game trail leading to the first spring. Emerging from the ground at the base of the ridge, Hillside Spring forms a pool the size of a bathtub, attracting deer, elk, bears, and wild turkeys. Sometimes. The pool's meager overflow trickles a hundred yards down a narrow grassy lane, then fans out and disappears back into the ground. Along that brief seep-line lie several shallow puddles that bull elk favor for wallows. On this day, happily, Hillside Spring was flowing – yet, unhappily, the area was naked of sign: no fresh tracks, droppings, antler rubs, or wallows.

One hope down, two left to hope for.

On the way to the second pool the breeze stiffened to a wind, the sky segued rapidly from cobalt to gray to black, and within minutes the temperature plunged what felt on the thermometer of my naked arms like 20 degrees. Lightning winked and thunder rumbled afar in the west, moving quickly closer. Suddenly I was shivering and cursing myself for not having brought along a light jacket, or at least a long-sleeved shirt. "We'll just have to tough it out," I grumbled to Otis, stroking his big graying head so he'd know I was scolding myself, not him.

But ugly as the weather was acting, all such concerns were forgotten the moment we reached Elk Spring, whose knee-deep pool, usually clear as polished glass, was turgid with recently churned bottom-silt. From years of experience I knew this pool took about four hours to clear, so the action had been recent. Big, moist, split-hoof prints waffled the damp earth all around. And even in the rising wind, the gut-stirring stench of elk smelled bold and intoxicating. So, my cervid friends hadn't deserted the mountain after all, but were merely ...

Ssssssszzzzz ... Ka-Rakkk!!!

A jag of cloud-to-ground lightning boomed and sizzled so near that the hair on my neck went erect, leaving me momentarily blinded. I thought perhaps I was dead. An instant later came an explosion of thunder so painfully sharp that I slapped my hands to my ears and fell to my knees. For his part, Otis let out a howl — not the prolonged wolfish sort, but a howl, as I interpreted it, of absolute terror. Then, as if the nearby lightning strike had slashed open the belly of the sky, hail the size and consistency of marbles came blistering down. We sprinted for the iffy shelter of the nearest big fir tree, whose limbs formed an umbrella that touched the ground all around. As I dove in, Otis came right behind and crowded hard against me beneath the low tangle of boughs. Like me, he was shaking hard.

Cringing there, we were somewhat protected from the worst of the hammering hail – which, beyond our sylvan shelter, was quickly turning the formerly green forest world to white. Rapidly growing colder, I rummaged frantically through my fanny pack, praying that the big plastic garbage bag I'd rolled up and tossed in ages ago as emergency rainwear (sort of) was still serviceable.

And there it was, welcome as a Christmas bonus. With my belt knife I cut a head opening in the center of the bottom seam, then slashed armholes on either side and worked the delicate bag carefully down over my head and shoulders. While the impromptu poncho covered my torso to just above the knees, it left head, neck, arms, lower legs, and feet unprotected — if in fact you can call a garbage bag "protection."

Ironically, it occurred to me that if I were hunting rather than "just scouting," I'd be handsomely equipped with my big hunting pack stuffed with everything necessary to remain in the woods safely, and in relative comfort, through anything short of a prolonged blizzard – including especially a *real* rain suit or poncho. But who'd ever think of needing serious foul-weather gear when merely stepping out on a hot sunny summer afternoon for a few leisurely hours of snooping around? I am not well known as an optimist, yet this time I'd let complacency get the best of me. Now I was paying the price.

While the big tree blocked the worst of it, hail was hitting the ground outside our sylvan shelter so hard it bounced and rolled and slowly piled up into a ring all around us. Putting Otis between the tree and me, I did my best to protect my pal, who'd grown too old for such keen physical excitement. For a while, I'd packed one of those *el cheapo* plastic ponchos you can buy at discount stores for the price of a cheap cheeseburger. Although next to worthless for bowhunting, they're good insurance against hypothermia and general wet-weather misery. Moreover, they come in flat, compact packages and have hoods to help dull the sting of driving rain and hail. But I'd found even that too bulky for my small fair-weather fanny pack, and in a tantrum of streamlining had tossed it out some time before in favor of the trash bag. Now, though better than nothing, I'd have to rate the baggie's overall performance as, well, garbage.

After several more minutes, the hail finally softened and turned to slushy rain. Should we stay put or run for it? Storms like this could blow through in minutes, or last for hours. My bare arms were the biggest problem, and I was starting to shake — not a good sign. Ironically, at such times being "fit" can work against a body. I am thin (the Marines, when I was one of them, called it "lean and mean," though I feel a lot

In the mountains a perfect day can become the perfect storm in minutes.
(Thomas Downing)

more meek than mean just now), with low blood pressure, and so have little built-in resistance to cold. If we didn't get moving soon, I knew, I might find myself unable to move ever again. Another concern, hunkered below a natural lightning rod as we were, was the calamitous electrical storm, which had mellowed only a little. Nothing for it but to forgo checking the third spring and scurry down the mountain fast as our six legs could carry us, Otis and me, tails tucked in miserable humility.

But perhaps we were too late already. As we slogged through brush as wet as the underside of an outhouse, the wind howling and cold like God's own swamp cooler, my chills ran so deep that I began losing feeling in fingers and toes and stumbling every few steps. To say I didn't feel a bit, well, "concerned" would be lying.

Even so, I was not yet in critical danger, and I knew it. I could and by-gosh *would* make the downhill miles to shelter and safety in an hour of determined trudging, easily beating darkness and the onset of irre-coverable hypothermia – unless, of course, I were to sprain an ankle or break a leg or jam a sharp stick into my belly while thrashing half-blind through the drowning woods or become disoriented in the downpour and growing fog or ... like waking nightmares, I recalled with a jolting shiver several other, far more adventurous pre-season scouting trips I'd taken in years past, probing far into rugged, unfamiliar territory equally unprepared as I was this day. I cringed to think what might have hap-pened on any of *those* occasions had Big Weather come swooping in with claws extended, hiding landmarks, chilling me to the marrow, making finding dry wood and starting a survival fire all but impossible.

Hypothermia: death by a thousand shivers.

As we slogged on, I glanced down in envy of Otis's ability to shake off accumulated water every several seconds, before it could soak through to the hide and chill him – exactly as I've seen elk, deer, bears, moose, and caribou do. I just wished he wouldn't shake so much of it onto me. My cotton cap was long since sopped and the icy water draining from it followed my neck like a funnel through the head-slit in the garbage bag, where it split into double torrents down back and chest, past my belt to the delicate bits beyond. My arms by now were purple and pimpled with cold and bleeding from limb-slashes that grew in number and se-verity as we sped miserably along. My legs were drenched from hips to ankles, and my low-topped hiking shoes squished like sponges with ev-ery treacherous step. And even faster than I had feared, my trashy "rain suit," like my arms, was being shredded by the grabby fingers of passing brush. I was inching ever deeper into hypothermia. Only rapid walk-ing was keeping me alive, and that walking was increasingly difficult to manage. If only I could sit down for a moment and rest.

But you do what you must when you must, or you lose it all. So I shouldered all fear aside and just kept going, and going.

By the time we finally reached the cabin – *Hallelujah!* – I was shaking so violently I could hardly stand. A hot shower was heaven; it felt like, and in point of fact *was*, life restored. For Otis, a good bath-toweling and a big bowl of kibbles worked the same wonders.

While the pyrotechnics moved gradually on eastward across the big Divide, the rain continued throughout the night.

On reflection, I don't think I realized, even at the worst of times, just how very dicey things had become that day. And adding proverbial insult to injury, it would have been eternally embarrassing to die for reasons so brilliantly dumb. And especially so while "just scouting."

It has long been said, and we'd best never forget, that the mountains don't give a damn.

CHAPTER 4

Screwups

Sooner or Later...

Mid-November, and I've had an elk in the freezer since the September bow season. Now, itching to hunt again, I'm doing something I very rarely do — two somethings in fact — hunting deer, and doing it with a rifle rather than a bow. With time running out in the brief buck-only rifle season, I'm sneaking through a narrow pinon-juniper tree row, glassing an adjacent hayfield for deer. Hardly a wilderness hunt, as I'm accustomed to when chasing elk. Low, pastoral, thinly-treed ranch country is where the deer are this time of year here in southwest Colorado, so I'm here too.

I started this hunt just yesterday, and with a bow, and as bowhunter's luck would have it, last evening I saw deer here by the dozens, including a matched pair of fine fat 4x4's (I have a buck-only tag), but both of them far beyond bow range and utterly unapproachable across a hundred acres of knee-high brome grass. And because this is a rifle season I'm required to wear blaze orange even though bowhunting, further complicating matters.

And so it has come to pass that this morning I'm toting a rifle, looking to make meat and get it done with: shopping more than hunting as I know it. And of course there are no deer in sight. By the time I reach the end of the mile-long wood row that corners the sprawling pasture like an L, I'm ready to call it quits; go home and do some work; maybe try again this evening.

And then the buck appears, all head and neck, rising like some Loch Ness creature from a flaxen sea of standing hay, 200 yards away. No trophy by any book standard, but a table trophy to me. Although he's belly-deep in grass, his vitals are fully visible. This, then, is it. Resting my Remington in the fork of a pinon (pronounced "pinyon") snag, I cross the hairs mid-chest on the broadside 4x4, consciously relax and squeeze.

When the ought-six barks, the buck turns and looks my way. Nothing more.

Huh? Granted, 200 yards is a stretch for someone who shoots a rifle as little as I have in recent years. But I visited the range only yesterday, confirming my 4X scope is sighted an inch high at a hundred yards. And I have a solid rest.

Whatever the problem, the deer seems willing to give me a second go. My pulse pounding hard, expecting the buck to disappear any moment, I lift the rifle from the tree crotch in order to work the bolt, return to rest, and search anxiously for the buck — and there he stands: same spot, same pose, still staring my way. This time I hold a little higher, squeeze even more carefully, and he falls like a bucket of bricks.

Thanks to a flooded and partly frozen irrigation ditch between us, I can't go straight to the buck – invisible now that he's down and out in the waving grass – but must retrace my route, a mile and more, back past the ranch house where my truck is parked.

When I get there, the landowner, an amiable bearded Harley type, is outside waiting, having heard my shots. Together we hop in my truck and four-wheel it out across the pasture and straight to the buck – which we find stone dead, centered through the heart and lungs.

"Perfect shot," Larry offers by way of congratulations.

"Well," I start to reply ... but am distracted mid-sentence by the sound of something big, thrashing around in the grass, and not so far away. Curious, we step over and find ... a second buck, spine-shot; down but not quite dead.

Knowing intuitively – certainly not consciously – that this is my doing, my fault, I hear myself moaning "Oh no! I'm sorry!" The spontaneous apology isn't intended for Larry, but for the wounded buck. After running to the truck for my rifle and dropping a round in the tube, I place the muzzle behind the trembling animal's ear and send him beyond the reach of pain or fear.

That heartbreaking chore accomplished, I turn to Larry and say exactly what I'm thinking: "I *know* I shot twice at the *same* buck."

Recalling every detail I can of those adrenaline-fogged moments, and near as I can figure it, these two bucks, pals and virtual twins, were bedded together in the brome grass. One stood and I shot, taking him in the heart and lungs – a "perfect" shot, perhaps, but not always instantly lethal as I know from long experience both as hunter and hunting guide. Blissfully unaware of his fate – this must be how it was – the heart-hit buck waited until the few moments I had my eye off the scope to collapse. In that same awful interval, the second buck, bedded only a few feet away, stood, effectively taking his partner's place and pose, broadside and staring my way. Seeing one and the same buck in my mind and scope, my higher "follow-up" shot had crushed the second deer's spine.

"I just wish to hell," I tell Larry, "I'd stayed in bed this morning."

The rancher, who I hardly know at all, attempts to console me — or perhaps to scold me for my self-pity – offering that "You're not the only one this sort of thing has happened to. We all make mistakes. Try as we might, sometimes it can't be helped."

Having nothing to say to that, I say nothing.

"Well, anyhow," Larry continues ... "what you gonna do now?"

Good question.

"First," I hear myself saying, "I take care of the meat. Then I go see Cary."

Larry, who's utterly innocent but caught in the middle, nods in silent agreement.

Cary Carron is the local game warden – more properly, District Wildlife Manager – for the Colorado Division of Wildlife. Over the years that we've horse-camped and hunted together, Cary has become a valued friend whose respect I'd hate to lose. But that's a risk I'll have to take. I'll explain how it happened, as straight as I can. I'll probably get a ticket – maybe, if I'm lucky, just a warning citation, this being my first-ever "wildlife offense." One buck will be confiscated; that's the law. The other I'll give to Larry, having suddenly lost my stomach for venison. No favors expected, asked or likely to be given. No skeletons left to rattle accusingly in anyone's closet.

Here in Colorado, as in most states, the accidental killing of a big game animal, assuming you promptly turn yourself and the animal in, is a hand-slap infraction. Abandonment of meat, however, is a handcuff felony. Even if you can live with the lie, it's a fool's bet to try.

Later, as we load the bagged meat quarters and twin antlered heads into my truck, Larry says again, "Don't let it bother you too much, bud. Sooner or later, it happens to every hunter. You're no exception."

"Yes," I say, "I suppose it does. I suppose I'm not."

But rather than making me feel better, as Larry is trying to do, this truism makes me even more morose. If "everybody" makes such deadly mistakes from time to time ... God, what a waste!

Ironically, warden Carron, who lives nearby, is out hunting with his daughter when I arrive. With the help of Cary's son, Doug, I unload the heads and bagged meat of both deer in their garage, whose stone-cold concrete floor will serve well as a temporary meat locker.

It's late when Cary finally calls. I explain what happened and how I think it came about, and as expected, he's calm and understanding, echoing Larry's admonition to quit beating up on myself. "Sorry to say," says Cary, "this sort of thing happens all the time."

Next morning, I drive back to Cary's house and he "writes me up," explaining that it's mandatory for the offense. The paltry $67 fine, however, reflects the CPW's understanding that honest, self-confessed mistakes, no matter how stupid, aren't the same as intentional wildlife crimes. While he's writing, my old friend recounts a similar "screw-up" of his own.

A few years before, Cary's son Doug, then 16, had drawn a doe pronghorn permit, and Cary went along for the hunt. After a good hard stalk, the father-son team finally got into range of a browsing herd. Selecting a doe standing a little off from the others, Doug hunkered down and took the 150-yard shot. The doe's only reaction was to stop eating and look up.

The next instant, the whole herd broke into a panicked retreat, concealing Doug's doe amongst the swirling mass. Convinced he'd missed, Cary urged his son to shoot again.

Thinking fast, Doug selected a doe that had broken away from the running herd, supposing she could be the one he'd shot at and possibly wounded. This time, at the rifle's crack the doe went down. The hunters were elated – until, moments later, after the dust had settled, they spotted a second doe lying dead on the prairie.

"When we went over to check it out," Cary recalls, "we determined that the first doe had been lung-shot but didn't know it right off. In that brief space of time, we screwed up."

As a wildlife law-enforcement officer, Cary was now in a pretty fix. A lesser man, more concerned about his career and public image than about the negative life-lesson a cover-up would teach his son, might have walked away. Instead, the Carrons field-dressed both does, drove to town, turned themselves and the animals in and took their ticket.

Now, as he hands me my own ticket to sign, Cary recounts yet another such story: A few years back, a CPW warden from another part of the state, under similar circumstances as Doug and Cary's, killed two prongies while hunting in his own patrol district. "It sure felt strange," he later told Cary, "to write myself a ticket."

Memory thus primed, I've recalled a third CDOW employee confession, told to me by a biologist who's ethics, like Cary's, are impeccable: A muley buck appeared atop a hill. The hunter shot and the buck disappeared ... only to reappear moments later: same buck, same spot. Assuming he'd missed, the hunter shot again and watched the buck take a tumble. When the off-duty biologist walked up the hill and peeked over the rim – yep, you got it – there lay twin bucks.

"Sooner or later, it happens to everyone."

Nor are such humbling hunting mishaps limited to multiple kills. I once knew a fellow who, back when he was young and overzealous, shot an illegal doe at a hundred yards with iron sights on a foggy mountain morning, certain her big ears were antlers. More recently, another young friend killed his first bull elk the wrong way, with a cow-only permit, as the smallish yearling stood in shadow 150 yards away, its slender seven-inch spikes hidden behind erect ears. Yet another would-be honorable hunter tumbled a hen turkey he just knew was a jake, mistaking a broken breast feather for a beard. And so on: killing a potential record-book buck whose massive antlers, protruding above high brush, "transformed" him into the bull elk the hunter was permitted for ... killing two elk with one shot, a calf unseen behind its mother ... and more.

And you, no doubt, can lengthen the list, if not from personal experience, from stories others have told.

And here's the really scary bit: If such mishaps now and again befall even those of us who try damn hard to play by the rules, what sort of bloody mayhem must "they" – hunting's legions of care-less slobs – be wreaking on a regular basis, then boasting about in public?

No wonder the "antis" hate us.

Life isn't perfect. Yet, if we keep always in mind that those aren't video targets out there, but living, sentient creatures we're throwing hot lead and sharp steel at, and that once the trigger is touched or the string released, there's no turning back – if we remind ourselves of the deadly seriousness of our actions every time we prepare to shoot, we can often, if not always, prevent the heartbreak and shame of "screw-ups."

Working toward that happy end, from this day on I foreswear to ...

1. Take more time and scan more carefully behind and all around apparently "lone" animals – looking for ears, antlers, legs – doing all I can be sure nothing is lurking unseen.

2. Assume I've hit every animal I shoot at, and not shoot again until I determined absolutely otherwise.

3. Make absolutely certain the animal I'm shooting at is the animal specified on my license: sex, age, species.

4. Never ever shoot at an animal in a group of animals – both for fear of killing or wounding non-target animals (via pass-throughs or misses), and because it's often impossible to keep track of a shot-at animal and determine its condition when the whole herd explodes.

5. Never shoot at a running animal, or at one that's not positively identifiable as legal game.

6. When rifle (as opposed to bow) hunting, I'll never again aim for a heart/lung hit — which has proven repeatedly to be too often too slow to kill – but rather hold high and forward to break the shoulder blade, simultaneously anchoring the animal and venting its lungs for a slam-dunk kill.

7. Make no more marginally long shots, which 200 yards qualifies as for most of us, even with a rest. Additionally, the closer the animal, the better you can observe its actions and surroundings before and after the shot. And too (here's the traditional bow-hunter speaking), if we're not close enough to an animal we kill to have penetrated its sensory defense system, then we're not hunting but only shooting, sniping, executing.

8. And most important of all – if I should ever again suffer another "screw-up," I'll (again) obey the dictates of law and honor: save the meat and face the music.

Finally, this seems a proper place to state my belief that all wildlife law enforcement officers should be, or at least once have been, active hunters. Those who lack personal hunting experience, yet must often make fine-line judgments of hunters, their actions and words, are handicapped by a critical lack of intimate personal knowledge. An essential empathy, available only through the college of hard knocks and the university of understanding, is missing. And without empathy, it's all too easy to become jaded and view even honest mistakes as wanton criminal acts – when, in fact, as you and I and all experienced hunters sadly know ...

Sooner or later, we *will* screw up.

CHAPTER 5

Sixth Sense...
or Nonsense?

There's a natural mystic flowing through the air.

—Bob Marley

The other day I received an intriguing email from my Arkansas hunting buddy and fellow campfire philosopher, Joseph "Jody" Smotherman. Before I share Jody's strange but true experiences (with his permission, of course), you should know that this gentleman is highly educated (Doctor of Pharmacology with a master's in Divinity on the side) and as solid as granite; the likelihood of BS here is zero.

Jody's story:

"This afternoon, I walked into my backyard woods [200 acres] to collect fallen acorns for my three young daughters to plant, and to have a casual look-around before the evening whitetail hunt. While out there, I suddenly felt a strong premonition that a coyote was watching me. In my mind's eye I could clearly 'see' the animal, standing and looking at me from 40 yards or so and to the southwest, upwind. The strange thing is that I hadn't looked up for probably a minute or two when this 'vision' struck. I had been squatted down collecting acorns with my full attention on the ground inches from my face. I don't recall having seen or heard *anything* to tip me off. Anyhow, of course I looked up — and sure enough, a large coyote stood right where I had 'seen' him. The dog and I stared at each other briefly before he loped away. Stranger yet, Dave, is that I'd had a near-identical experience with a bobcat a couple of years before, also here on my land. Then too, I 'knew' both where and what the animal was before I saw it. Have you ever had eerie moments like these in the outdoors? Do these surreal experiences owe to my deep physical and spiritual connection to my backyard woods? To some voo-doo supernaturalism? Insanity? Who knows?"

Does any of this sound like *déjà vu* to you? Sure does to me, though my "sixth sense" episodes have never been as precise as Jody's. Whether sixth sense or nonsense, such apparently paranormal events (not scientifically explainable, or not yet scientifically explained) happen to us more often than rarely ... out there in the shadowy, sometimes spooky wilds.

Psychic Staring Effect (PSE) is the term researchers attach to the creepy feeling of being watched by an unseen entity, human or otherwise. PSE, in turn (sorry about all the acronyms), is a subset or aspect of ESP (Extrasensory Perception). But no matter the tag, when it comes to such "truth is stranger than fiction" encounters between humans and animals, I think there's something to it — something having naught to do with voodoo supernaturalism but rather facilitated, quite naturally, by ancient sensory survival instincts. Such instincts logically and with good reason would have evolved through thousands of human and pre-human generations spent living and dying among fellow wildings, some of which we ate and others, lots of others, that killed and gnawed on us.

Following this logical line of evolutionary speculation, it's perhaps no coincidence that in both instances Jody's watchers were predators

... small, nonthreatening (to humans) predators, but predators none-theless. And isn't it logical to presume that predators, perhaps due to their furtive body language, put out different "vibes" than prey species, and further, that it's precisely those vibes to which early humans long ago developed a hyper-acute, almost *extra*-sensory sensitivity? I mean, how would it benefit the survival of our ancestors and our species-in-the-making to experience premonitions of being watched by a rabbit or a robin? Or even a giant ground sloth?

All this makes solid sense to an open and evolutionarily informed mind ... until we get to the part where Jody's reading of the bobcat and coyote's speculative "vibes" was so precise as to accurately reveal their species as well as locations.

My pragmatically playful conclusion is that our PSE episodes in the woods are the products of a little-understood evolved ability within the human brain to tally-up almost microscopically subtle clues from the five physical senses, thus creating a *virtual* sixth sense. These clues — and here's the "extra" sensory part — are so small and fleeting that they fail to register consciously. Yet they are duly noted in the subconscious where they are stashed, at least in short-term memory. When enough clues accrue that snick together like puzzle pieces, they are combined to produce a synthesized Psychic Staring Effect that can stand our hair on end (those who still have any) and leave us, as with Jody, to wonder if we've finally gone utterly insane.

Tangentially, if not directly related to my amateurish postulations regarding PSE owing substantially to subconscious rather than con-scious workings of the senses and brain, ongoing research into the true, deeply disguised nature of human free will in decision-making – wear-ing such daunting monikers as "the Newtonian World Machine vs. Quantum Indeterminism" – concludes much the same: that an over-whelming percentage of our "conscious decisions" in fact have already been made subconsciously before we even "think them to ourselves."

See, for instance, Harvard neuroscientist Sam Harris' compact and intriguing tome *Free Will* (NY, 2012, Free Press/Simon &Schuster).

Restated: Until such time as scientific method confirms or denies what seems obvious, until such time, empirical evidence and logic point to PSE as being a synthesized sum of sensory inputs so super-subtle as to be overlooked by the often-distracted conscious mind. (My friend Jody, you'll recall, was thinking about acorns and his three lovely little daughters.) Yet these nearly invisible clues are somehow registered and matched-up by an undistracted subconscious: A fleeting peripheral glimpse of a miniscule movement here, a faint scent on the breeze there, a tiny uncharacteristic rustle among wind-stirred leaves (and Jody, it's worth noting, wears the sharpest woods ears I've ever witnessed in action) ... all these ghostly micro-clues crunched together in our subconscious personal computers to generate an unnerving "Heads-up!" alert that in the long ago – and even today in some places and circumstances – could save your bacon, or mine.

"Real and surreal at the same time," is how Jody concluded his retelling, and I think that pretty well nails it. While there's definitely something mystical, as brother Bob Marley described it, "flowing through the air" in the world we inhabit, it's a purely *natural* mystic, neither sixth sense nor nonsense.

CHAPTER 6

Elkheart
and the Indian Guide
By Thomas Downing

DP note: *I did not write the following story. Yet it recounts one of my most memorable elk hunts ever, thus easily rating inclusion here. Thomas Downing, in his first published writing, did an outstanding job of recalling that hunt, our hunt, for* Traditional Bowhunter Magazine *readers. My thanks to Thomas for allowing me to fold these good memories into this collection.*

The previous two days of meat-packing had been exhausting. The sweat dripping from my forehead and my burning legs and lungs were sharp reminders that bowhunting elk in the high country is never easy. I reached the trailhead first and gratefully shucked the heavy pack from my back. This was our third and final load of meat and antlers. My father, Joe Downing, aka Pop, was a few minutes behind me and as I awaited his arrival I smiled in appreciation of the man and his toughness. Even at 68, this former Airborne paratrooper just keeps on trucking.

I'd been fortunate enough to kill an animal on the final Thursday of the 2009 Colorado archery elk season. I cow-called in and shot the satellite bull two hours' hike downhill from the trailhead in one of Colorado's magnificent public lands roadless areas, where the motorized crowds not only can't go, but we and the elk couldn't even hear them;

we were that far in. It had taken Pop and me the better part of two days to pack the animal out. And now, just after arriving home, totally exhausted and dreaming of a hot shower and bed, the phone rang.

"Hey T, this is Dave, what's going on? Have you been into the elk again since we last talked?"

I told Dave about my close-quarters bull, shot from five yards, and our grueling pack-out. He congratulated me and praised my father for his grit and determination, concluding "I hope I can do as well when I'm his age." Dave, who is only five years younger than Pop, went on to explain that the drainage he'd been hunting had several resident bulls that throughout the month had been bugling their heads off. But now, after three weeks of what he calls "playing with my food" and "half-assed trophy hunting," he was anxious to take "any edible elk," yet it wasn't working out. Stalking the vocal bulls in dense cover had provided Dave with some thrilling close encounters but no solid shot opportunities. Consequently, across the month my friend had come to know "his" bulls so well he could identify individuals by their bugles and predict with confidence their general whereabouts at any given time.

"Look," Dave said, cutting to the chase, "I know Joe is still here and hasn't yet taken an animal and there's only one day left in the hunt, but is there any chance you can call for me tomorrow morning? At this point it seems my only chance to make meat."

My energy immediately returned and I was intrigued about the possibility of calling in another bull. I was also excited because I had never elk hunted with "Elkheart." We'd backpack-camped and chased timberline deer with our longbows in the past but despite several years of talking about it, we'd never hunted elk together. Dave mainly hunts alone and I spend the majority of my elk time with my father. I put Dave on hold for a moment and I asked Pop if he was willing to sacrifice the final morning of the season.

"Son, if we were to kill another elk it would likely take us another two days to get it out and I have to leave for British Columbia on Monday morning. I'm not willing to put all of that on you. I think you should take this opportunity to hunt with Dave." I got back on the phone and we hashed out our strategy for Sunday morning, the final day of a four-week season during which Dave had hunted every day but one.

In my experience, on the last day of a season magical opportunities often present themselves. As I watched for Dave's headlights winding up my driveway early Sunday morning, I felt confident that this day would bear good luck. Dave was confident as well. As we pulled in to the trailhead, Dave gave me a quick update on the bulls.

"The herd bull, with most of the local cows, hangs out along a timbered ridge near the top of the mountain to the north and bugles sporadically all day long. But he refuses to leave his cows and I've considered it too risky to try and stalk him with all those eyes and noses on guard. There are several satellite bulls working around the big herd, plus a lone, deep-voiced "shirker" bull that beds on the side hill to the left of the drainage; he's there every day but isn't much of a singer. For whatever reason I think he's ducking out on the rut this year."

I was amazed how precisely Dave knew where each of the bulls would be and even something of their individual personalities. He knew every wrinkle on the local landscape from the elk's point of view and had been extremely careful not to let the animals know they were being hunted.

As the cherry glow of dawn brightened and we made our way quietly uphill, I reflected on why Dave had asked me to hunt with him this day. He's killed more elk than I have, so what could I possibly bring to the table for this "Man Made of Elk?" But of course I knew. While Dave employs various methods he always errs on the side of caution and consequently, he rarely calls, as he confesses, "Because it backfires on me more often than it works." To the contrary, I'm an aggressive hunter and while I share Dave's disdain for bugling in most situations today, I rely heavily on cow calling, primarily with my voice.

We walked in silence up the drainage. When we arrived at a bench covered with lime-green aspen saplings growing so thick we could see only a few feet into the hardwood jungle, I whispered "Let's give it a go from here." Dave nodded and I began my process of mentally becoming a lonely cow elk walking through the woods in search of a friendly bull. Sometimes I break twigs to simulate a heavy-hoofed animal and occasionally I'll pull a clump of grass out of the ground or tear aspen leaves off branches as I mew and chirp. On this magical morning, all it took was a couple of sweet calls.

Almost instantly the herd bull bugled back from well up the drainage, precisely where Dave predicted he would be. His bugling prompted another bull to answer from the left side of the timber and down lower, closer to us. Dave whispered, "That's the bull that spends his entire time over there and rarely bugles." While Dave had stalked to within bow range of Mr. Silent a couple of times, the aspen tangles hadn't even allowed him a glimpse of the recluse, much less a shot.

After a few more calling sequences, the canyon rang with the bugles of six bulls! Agreeing that we needed to find a shooting lane to set up in, and fast, we crept on up the hill until we reached another small bench rising to a dark-timbered ridge to the east. Again, the fire-rejuvenated aspen sapling jungle limited the view. Yet there was a significant shooting lane leading toward the ridge to our right, from which the nearest bull was threatening to appear at any moment. I announced I was going to stay put and call from a little depression that provided a discreet view along the lane toward the bull. Dave nodded in agreement and moved ahead through the opening to disappear behind a burnt standing tree just downwind of the lane. If the nearest bugler, only some 50 yards away but invisible in the dense dark timber, should come toward my calls, he'd pass by Dave within a few yards for a slam-dunk broadside.

Every time the hung-up bull bugled, I answered him with two or three chirps. Other bulls farther up the drainage would then sound off and you could *feel* the tension between them in the chilly morning air. I live for these wild and unpredictable moments and felt certain I could lure the nearest bull to Dave's waiting arrow.

But that plan went winging out the window when a beautiful 5x5 walked out of the aspens headed straight for where I assumed Dave was crouched in ambush. This new bull hadn't bugled to signal his approach and came from the direction we least expected, below us. I watched the bull intently as he moved closer to Dave, who, I'd later learn, wasn't set up for an animal coming from that direction and was caught effectively in the open, kneeling, with no cover either in front or behind him along this new bull's line of sight. Not certain where Dave was set up and whether or not he'd seen the approaching bull, I quit calling.

Stopping occasionally to gaze casually around him, seemingly oblivious to the nearby bugler in the woods, the 5x5 kept walking forward until abruptly, he spun around and trotted back off in the direction he'd come from. I called several times in hopes of stopping the retreating bull, all the while wondering what had happened. Had he seen Dave? Had Dave seen him? We had the wind perfectly, so I didn't think he could have smelled us. After a short trot the bull slowed and walked out of sight. Had my calling calmed him down? Was he still around?

After a while Dave appeared, walking gingerly toward me. "That was *incredible*," he whispered. "I thought that goofy bull was going to step on me; just crazy!"

"What happened," I asked? "I could see the bull, but I couldn't see you."

"Let's sit down and chill-out for a minute."

For a while we sat in silence as the bugling all around gradually slacked. Finally, Dave said, "I think it will be fine, but I'm worried that I didn't reach full draw before I released."

Dumbfounded, I blurted out: "You got a *shot*?"

Dave just looked at me and smiled, and then my questions came boiling out: "Did you see where your arrow hit? How close was the bull when you shot? Do you think he's down nearby?"

"Because he wasn't bugling, I think this may be the recluse bull. He was no more than six feet away, towering over me and still coming. I knew the bubble was about to burst and decided to see if I could draw and get a good sight picture before he bolted. I knew he'd spin and run. And a shot on a spinning animal is rarely a good shot because the lateral motion complicates aiming and limits penetration; normally I wouldn't even consider it. But at *six feet*? And I had confidence in my arrow set-up with a heavy shaft and good FOC and a first-rate single-bevel head. Not to mention last-day insanity! I mean, it was try for a shot or let the bull step on me or whatever it was he had in mind. If it didn't feel right when I drew and he spun I wouldn't release. But it did feel right and I did release and my arrow caught him mid-chest — not a perfect low-forward heart shot, but a good solid mid-lung hit nonetheless with maybe half-shaft penetration on a 30-inch arrow."

We agreed that since we hadn't seen or heard the bull go down we should have lunch and wait a full hour before following up. As we ate and talked in whispers, I resumed calling, though less urgently now. Once again the resident bulls responded with a passionate concert, helping to distract us from the gut-churning concerns Dave shared with me: Had the bull left a blood trail? Would we be able to recover him promptly? Or at all? And bottom line, Dave confessed his worry, was that gorgeous animal suffering because his split-second decision to take the rushed shot had after all been unwise and therefore unintentionally unethical? "Man," he concluded, "I *hate* myself when they don't go down in sight and I thought I'd solved that problem years ago."

When we finally got to work, I headed straight to where I'd last seen the bull walking away, while Dave returned to where he'd taken

Elkheart with his Six-Foot bull (Thomas Downing)

*Thomas Downing, aka Elkheart's Indian guide, with his bull of the year
(Joe Downing)*

the shot to search for blood. Right away I found Dave's arrow lying on the ground, minus the broadhead. There was bright red lung blood up to half-shaft but the broadhead had come off, which likely meant it was still in the animal. The excitement was palpable when I showed the arrow to Dave, and we shared a sigh of relief, agreeing that 15 inches of penetration was enough to have completely penetrated one lung and likely gotten into the off-side lung as well. Yet, there was no blood trail.

"I'm gonna check out that little thicket of aspen saplings down there by the gully," Dave announced. "They tend to head downhill when they're badly hurt, and no farther than they have to. If you stay here on this rise, you'll be able to see if he sneaks out ahead of me."

I liked Dave's plan. From the vantage where we stood I had a panoramic view of both sides of the drainage and if the bull came out I would definitely see him. With a growing sense of relief, suddenly I noticed the beauty of our surroundings and that the morning sun, still low, was shining bright on the aspen leaves and the grass glistened with morning dew. Life was good and my fingers were crossed that Dave would find his bull dead in the aspens.

As Dave moved out with an arrow on the string, in the event a follow-up shot was needed, I continued to cow call, watching everything around me intently. Several minutes had passed uneventfully when I heard a small noise to my left and looked to see a nontypical 6x7 headed right toward me. At almost the same moment, Dave reappeared beside me. "Look at that bull," I exclaimed and pointed. Dave looked but said nothing as the bull continued its approach, now almost in bow range. At that point I stopped calling and the nontypical stared at us for a while before melting back into the forest, not the least spooked.

"That was a *nice* bull!" I declared. "High, narrow rack; you don't see bulls like that every day."

Any other time, such a rare encounter would have Dave as excited as I was. Instead, showing only concern on his white-bearded face, Dave was single-minded, reporting that he hadn't found any blood, much less the dead elk he'd expected. And then he gave me a look I had never seen in him before — pure focused intensity — and declared that yet another walk down into the jungle was called for because "It was so thick and impenetrable in places I could have missed something. He *has* to be in there."

So off he went again while I stayed put on my lookout perch. No sooner had Dave disappeared back into the dense little patch of aspens than a bull came walking out, swaying heavily from to side like a moose in rut. I watched the bull for only a moment before he simply disappeared, as if God had plucked him from the earth. I was stunned. I bird-whistled to Dave and when he returned I pointed out where I'd last seen the wobbling bull. At just this instant yet another bull, a wide-antlered 6x6, appeared, bugling full-bore from a hundred yards below us and maybe half of that from where I'd last seen Dave's bull.

After watching this latest miraculous appearance for a moment, Dave headed off toward where the wobbler had disappeared. For a short while all was quiet, with the notable exception of the new bull so close below. Then I heard Dave call out with surprising calmness: "T! We're done. Come on down."

Yet again on this amazing morning I felt the electric surge of adrenaline as I ran down toward Dave. He had walked right to the fallen bull. To say that I was more excited than Elkheart would be an understatement; even though we'd recovered the bull promptly, the "less than instant" kill clearly bothered him a lot. I hugged my old friend in congratulations and then we sat without speaking for several minutes, admiring and mourning the fallen prey. What a beautiful, big-bodied bull! I said a silent prayer for the animal and for the blessing of this piece of still-wild elk country. After a while we took the requisite "hero" pictures and I even shot a brief video on my digital camera. Dave was incredibly calm, personifying the wily old veteran he is.

Dave's arrow had in fact penetrated only one lung and the bull had bled completely internally, which explained, as so often happens with one-lunged elk, why there was no blood trail whatsoever. The lung, however, was pulverized to an extent neither of us had ever before seen caused by arrow or bullet, and enough blood was pooled in the chest cavity, as Dave noted, "for a man to drown in."

As we set about dressing out the animal I watched with fascination Dave's surgeon-like technique. I hadn't had a chance to resharpen my knives from dressing my own elk so hadn't brought one along that morning, relying on Dave to be amply prepared. But wouldn't you know it, Dave had forgotten his trusty Helle belt knife and was left to do the entire job with a little homemade backup blade and a folding bone saw.

As we worked, we stashed the meat in heavy cotton game bags, which we cached in the shade before heading back down the mountain to the truck, where we'd left our pack frames and more game bags. But it was early yet and the day was cool, so before beginning the pack-out grind we decided to return home for a good lunch — not that far, as we are mountain neighbors. I arrived at my house about noon, walked in and proudly showed my father, wife and two young sons the blood on my hands while describing the morning's hunt. When I asked Pop if he'd like to "share in the joys" of meat packing one more time, he eagerly accepted.

Back on the mountain, my father and I packed out two easy loads of meat —everything except the two hind quarters — while Dave stayed to finish the boning and trim work. For the final trip, Pop and I packed the remaining meat while Dave carried out the bull's skinned skull and antlers on his shoulders, explaining "I always carry the rack out myself; it's a tradition."

As we approached the truck for a final time, Dave smiled at me with open appreciation and said "You done *good*, my Indian guide! I have no doubt that I'd have gone meatless this year without your expert calling." Despite the fact that I'm only a quarter Navajo, Dave's half-joking "Indian guide" compliment meant a lot to me. While it was my Anglo father who'd introduced me to bowhunting, I've always felt that a key component of my passion for the hunt owes to the Native roots passed down from my full-blooded maternal grandmother.

Pop said it all when he proclaimed with a laugh: "Elkheart and his Indian guide!"

This last-day hunt had indeed been magic.

Elkheart learned the hard way about bugle pollution.
(Branson Reynolds)

CHAPTER 7

Bugle Pollution
Way too much of a (once) good thing

Old Fart: *Hold 'er right there, pilgrim!*

Greenhorn: *Huh? Where are ye?*

Old Fart: *Make a fine target, pilgrim. Empty yer hands!*

Greenhorn: *Who ... ?*

Old Fart: *I'm Bear Claw Chris Lapp, blood kin to the grizzler that bit Jim Bridger's ass.*

Greenhorn: *I'm ...*

Old Fart: *I know who you are. You're the same dumb pilgrim I been hearin' for 20 days and smellin' for three... And you're molestin' my hunt!*

Like the crusty old mountain man Chris Lapp in the Robert Redford film *Jeremiah Johnson*, I reckon I too have seen enough seasons in the wild to be relegated to the ranks of Old Fart, and no going back. But Old Fartness has its gains, allowing a veteran hunter to preach from the pulpit of long experience if not necessarily wisdom. And from that pulpit this here Old Fart dares to declare that if you are among the hordes of hopeful Greenhorns who come bellowing into elk country each September with grunt tubes stuck in their faces like God's own cigars and ears ringing with their own faux bugles ... then you, Pilgrim, are molestin' my hunt!

As put by yet another senior woodsman E. Donnall Thomas: "During the Montana archery elk season, the principal function of elk calls has become to confirm the location of novice hunters to more experienced hunters and elk alike."

To summarize our complaint in advance: Bugling once was, and in the right hands and right circumstances still can be, among the most exciting and effective tools and techniques available to early season (rut) elk hunters, mostly but not exclusively during the September archery seasons. But bugling, like everything else in this crazy consumer society, has been over-marketed. Consequently, bugling has been overused and abused to the point that today it rarely works in the road- and motorized trail-accessible, heavily-hammered areas that most elk hunters are limited, or limit ourselves to. Far more often than not, in fact, frontcountry bugling backfires. That's why experienced hunters rarely if ever bugle these overcrowded days, leaving those who do bugle to be flagged — as Don Thomas notes, and the same is true here in Colorado — as novices who've spent more time watching the Outhouse Channel than out in the woods watching and learning about elk.

And so it is that excessive and unwise bugling, which most bugling is today, not only reduces the bugler's chances of getting close to elk, it also tips elk to the fact they're being hunted and makes them all the more wary, thus molesting the non-bugler's hunt as well. Worse yet, all that fake bugling promptly shuts up the real bulls, night as well as day. This unnatural silence, in turn, further complicates things for hunters while robbing both hunters and nonhunters of the inimitable joy of hearing real bulls sing.

And worst of all in this cascade of negative fall-out, though largely overlooked even by state wildlife agencies, is the fact that excessive fake bugling pressure that leads to a cessation of bugling by real bulls and thereby molests the carefully evolved elk breeding drama, which in its turn sets off a biological cascade of negative events that molests the long-term and even short-term (as when orchestras of fake bugling cause the rut to be disrupted and calves to be born late, leading in turn to an excessively high winterkill) biological health of the elk resource.

"Is it *really* all that bad?" asks the Greenhorn.

"Well," says the Old Fart, "slow down a minute and let me tell ya ..."

To those of us who've experienced the raging adrenaline high of having a screaming-hot bull come storming into breath-smelling range in response to our own fake bugling, bugling ever after defines elk hunting; it *is* elk hunting. Anything else is something else — and something a whole lot less. As an Old Fart I know this, having been there so often myself.

Which is why I so regret that we've gone and thrown our good thing away. And I am as guilty as anyone.

If bugling didn't play a key role in facilitating the survival and genetic refinement of the wapiti species, it would never have become a primary aspect of the elk reproductive ceremony. Out there in wild nature, gadgets and gimcracks that provide no survival or reproductive advantage to their owners and species — the proverbial tits on a motor — rarely last long. But bugling *did* evolve — that is, was selected by trial and error as an advantage to both individual buglers and their species, to become an integral part of male elkness. That was long, long ago. That bugling persists universally yet today among wapitoid species proves its tenacious worth.

On average, the annual wapiti rut in North America opens gradually beginning in mid-August, when antler growth is complete and bulls shed their velvet, and continues through early to mid October, by which time most eligible cows have been bred and, consequently, male testosterone levels plummet. (According to studies in Oregon and Colorado, actual breeding is concentrated in the last week of September and the first week of October.) Among the highest *known* purposes of bugling throughout the weeks-long hyperactive rut activity are advertising and stress reduction. As Olaus Murie, the father of modern elk biology, noted nearly a century ago (while time flies, facts last much longer) in the original *Elk of North America*:

"During the rut the bulls are in a turmoil of unrest. The physiological development at this period has produced a swollen neck and other sexual changes. The tremendous sexual urge and intense emotional state of the animal require definite expression. The elk cows are very evasive. The bulls are under terrific strain, and the bugling appears to be but a partial outlet for the pent-up feelings."

Of course, the only *fully* satisfying outlet for the "pent-up feelings [and] tremendous sexual urge and intense emotional state" of rutting bull elk is frequent copulation with a congeries of ripe and willing cows. And here too, via vocal advertising, bugling plays an essential role. As preeminent ethologist Valerius Geist summarizes in *Elk Country*:

"A bull's aim, clearly, must be to breed as many females as possible. The earlier he begins advertising, the more females he can 'convince' of his ability to provide effective shelter from harassment from young bulls, while teaching the cows that they are 'in control.' The more he advertises, the fewer females are likely to leave him, attracted and made curious about other actively bugling bulls. Consequently, the frequency of bugling coincides with the greatest amount of female activity. Also, it is in the bull's interest to out-advertise other bulls or to shut them up if it is in his power to do so. Thus, an advertising rival who happens to be nearby will be sought out and aggressively silenced. That's why bugling attracts bulls."

And, I would add, that's why wimpy, insecure fake bugling by hunters — sounding like an upstart — generally attracts more and bigger bulls than confident, boisterous bugling.

In the fascinating section "Adaptive Behavioral Strategies" in *North American Elk: Ecology and Management*, Geist further clarifies how and why bugling by mature bulls attracts and holds estrous females:

"To retain a loyal harem, a bull must differentiate his behavior from that of his rivals. His advertisements should condition the female positively to his presence. This makes bugling an integral part of the courtship sequence."

In sum, then, bugling by dominant bulls not only reduces the bugler's pent-up stress and intimidates lesser rivals, but, assuming he's the best candidate for the job, calms the cows as well.

Certainly, the observable fact that bugling attracts both rutting bulls and broody cows has never gone unnoticed by hunters. "By the time of Christ," reports Bart O'Gara in *North American Elk*, throughout Eurasia "mating calls were used by bowmen to locate or attract their prey," including especially the highly vocal red deer and wapiti. Whether European hunters brought their calling skills to North America with them, or learned from local Indians, it is known that by 1700 white hunters were making and using "whistles" to attract and kill rutting September bulls.

Looking even farther back, tens of thousands of years before elk whistles or other manufactured calls had likely been invented, prehistoric human hunters would have mastered the manipulation of their own vocal abilities to imitate various animal calls. Even today, among a talented few, this animal-ventriloquist's legacy lives on. In my home-

town of Durango, Colorado, Thomas Downing, an accomplished traditional bowhunter, for decades used his voice to create far more realistic
elk calls — bugles, chirps, mews and barks — than you'll hear from
any device on the market. (Alas, Thomas is a basketball junkie and blew
out his elk-calling voice one recent night by screaming for his favorite
team.)

Of course, such natural talent is ever in short supply. Consequently,
as fast as hunters could invent them, various artificial calls were brought
into play to facilitate luring game to within primitive-weapons range.
For one example, ethnographer E.T. Denig, in a 1930 report titled "Indian Tribes of the Upper Missouri," observed that "Whistles made of
wood like the mouthpiece of a clarinet are used [by the Assiniboine] to
call both deer and elk."

Among some American Indian tribes, hand-carved wooden elk
calls, in the forms of whistles and flutes, performed multiple duty as
musical instruments, art objects and magical icons (most often love
charms). In his survey of Indians and elk in *North American Elk*, histo-
rian Richard McCabe includes a photo of an elegantly carved Lakota
elk flute that not only imitates the whistling of a distant bugling bull, but
artfully depicts the animal's antlered head and open calling mouth with
evocative realism. (Similarly, I've had good luck getting rutting bulls to
answer plaintive high notes blown on a native American wood flute in
G flat.)

In modern times, the first truly effective, mass-produced and aggressively marketed bugling device appeared in the form of inexpen-
sive neoprene disks, aka diaphragm calls. The singular advantage of the
mouth-held diaphragm over other calling devices — an advantage that
assures the diaphragm's perpetual popularity among bowhunters — is
that it can be effectively employed hands-off, freeing the archer to draw
his (or increasingly, her) bow. For longer-distance work, the diaphragm
can be augmented with an amplifying and resonating "grunt" tube.

Finally, in talented hands (or mouths), the diaphragm is unequaled in the diversity of elk sounds it can make, from the raunchiest bugle to shocking barks to the mousiest little squeak.

Like so many other archers back in the early days of bugling, the instant I learned of this "revolutionary new way" to hunt bull elk in rut, I hurried to town to buy a pocketful of the little plastic half-moons. To save a few bucks, I salvaged a two-foot length of discarded vacuum-cleaner hose for a grunt tube. It was easy and it was fun ... in retrospect, way too much of both. But ignorance is always eager, and to the great annoyance of my wife and dogs, I practiced daily for weeks. Come September, I abandoned my traditional tactics of whitetail-style stalking and ambushing in favor of doing as the newborn crop of media bugling gurus advised, rushing from ridge-top to promontory and bugling my fool head off. And even back then in its heyday, with far fewer archers and muzzleloaders afield during September, and far fewer among us bugling at far less sophisticated bulls than today, sometimes it worked but mostly it didn't.

And what was the media "experts'" advice in such cases? Bugle all the more often and all the louder! Better yet, buy a new bugle every year in order to stay abreast of the "latest calling technology." The way this industry-twisted psychology works, even today, is that when our most flawless calls are answered with resounding silence, we can replace disappointment with hope simply by bugling some more.

And that, of course — blatant overconfidence and lack of self-restraint — is where it all went bad and remains counterproductive.

But *when* bugling did work, Pilgrim, and when it still works today, by damn it *works*. Sort of. Depending on lots of variables.

When I asked world deer expert Dr. Valerius Geist, "How do elk react when the early archery season opens and overnight they find themselves in a bugling-polluted landscape?" he responded:

"Who knows! Certainly not state-level wildlife managers, sad to say. And why *not*? Where are all the young biologists, their eyes and ears and noses glued to wild elk in an attempt to find out? I suspect that heavily hunted and relentlessly called-at elk sleep it off in impenetrable thickets and blow-down hells during the days, and do their breeding business at night. The bulls probably roam about more (not good!) and breed a few less females per estrus cycle (not good!). In case of doubt about the impact of excessive calling on the biological and social welfare of elk — and doubt is mostly all we have right now — the wisest policy would be to postpone the elk hunting season until the rut is done. Problem solved!"

Indeed, all problems of elk harassment by hunters during the rut — from over-bugling to incessant cow-calling to the annoying growl and whine of nervous ORVs, to just having so damn many of us out there ineptly sneaking around — all are products of allowing hunting during the rut. Given the ever-increasing numbers of us who want to hunt the rut with increasingly high-tech "primitive" bows and black powder rifles (which almost never use black powder any more), aided by a stellar array of space-age hunter's crutches like scent-proof camo clothing, increasingly realistic and easy to use game calls, low-light vision optics, "genuine cow-in-heat elk urine" extracted via inhumane procedures from captive elk, and so much more ... perhaps the day will come when enlightened game managers (it's possible!) will be forced to treat the increasingly negative symptoms of September hunting by curing the root cause.

Certainly, there are many degrees of options short of an all-out ban on rut-season hunting. Such halfway measure include limiting the number of early season licenses made available each year, particularly for bulls ... re-evaluating and redefining the concept of "primitive weapons" hunting in light of the current tendency for most early season "bow" hunters to carry "bows" equipped with muscle-saving high let-off cams, precision sights and the ability to launch toothpick-weight arrows twice as far twice as fast as the fastest of traditional (non-mechanical) recurves and longbows (whose users generally prefer heavier, thus more lethal, arrows). Similarly, "black powder" rifles today are capable of killing at ranges formerly restricted to modern smokeless-powder weapons.

Alas, experience shows that wherever and whenever state game agencies have attempted to place restrictions of any kind on early season hunters — from limiting licenses to shortening seasons to controlling firearms technology — hunter and industry outrage have won the day for self-righteous ignorance.

But if we want any semblance of *quality* in our future hunts ... if we want to maintain healthy, natural and huntable populations of wild wapiti far into the future ... if we want to honestly continue claiming that hunters were the original conservationists and remain among the most concerned and effective voices for wildlife welfare today and tomorrow ... *something* has to give. And let's hope sooner rather than later.

*This remote vernal pond provides both water and wallowing,
making it a perfect ambush site.*

CHAPTER 8

Ambush Tactics
A refresher course

No matter the animal we're hunting or the weapon we choose, we have but two fair- chase strategic options to work with: We either actively go after the game (by glassing, stalking or calling), or we find a comfy seat in a likely location, make like statues and let the game come to us.

Active versus passive. In the previous chapter we saw how tricky the active approach, via bugling, has become. Yet, its unarguably more fun for most hunters than warming a log with our butts. But personal preference – walking, calling or sitting – aside, which approach works best varies wildly according to the species being hunted, terrain and vegetation, weather, season (specifically, rut or not), on-site considerations and, perhaps most essentially, the hunter's experience, skills, physical abilities and patience level. And too, there's the good question of which "best" we're talking about: Best for bagging game, or best for personal satisfaction and fun times with the overall hunting experience? Best for producing product, or best for enjoying the process? Since most traditional bowhunters take the mature philosophical view that ranks enjoyment of *process* over a focused desire for *product*, "best" often equates to "what I'm in the mood for today." As primarily a predator of elk, I can say that I enjoy every fair-chase hunting method and use them *all* pretty much every year. To one degree and another.Yet across the years, most of my time has been spent, and most of my elk (and deer) have been killed, while sitting in ambush.

Here's what works for me ...

Do Your Homework

The first step in orchestrating an effective ambush is to predict accurately where the game will be and when. Let's assume you already know your way around the area you plan to hunt. Within that big ballpark, locating high-odds ambush sites involves learning to recognize, then thoroughly scouting, predictable game-concentrating features including (depending on species and terrain) wallows or scrape lines during the rut, morning and evening feeding areas, midday bedding areas, escape cover if the game is being pressured by hunters, saddles, ridges and other geographically delineated travel corridors, intersections of well-trafficked game trails, and, in dry conditions, water.

Planning a productive ambush also requires more than a passing knowledge of the daily habits and movements of your quarry, especially during fall, when so much (the rut, hunting seasons, seasonal migrations, weather) is going on. This requires head-down scouting and the ability to spot subtle spoor (droppings, trail and bed locations, rubs, wallows, etc.), determine the sign's approximate age and read it for such critical information as what food sources are being utilized (acorns or other nuts, browse, forage, etc.), which water holes are favored, which trails animals are using to approach and leave feeding and watering areas, dominant wind patterns at various times of day, whether a particular set-up will have you sitting in shade with the sun to your back, which you want, or looking into a blinding sun at the time of day you'll be there; and finally – all of this and a whole lot more having been carefully considered – making solid judgments about the choicest locations for ambush hides, whether to perch in a tree or hunker on the ground, and how best to come and go without leaving a scent trail loud as a burglar alarm.

In sum, effective ambush hunting requires (excuse the "obsolete" term) concertedly applied *woodsmanship*.

Where water is scarce, it's hard to beat isolated waterholes as ambush "bait," especially small pools that concentrate animals within stickbow range of your hide. In good habitat in most years, food is readily abundant, but throughout most of the American West, water is predictably precious. Magnify this scarcity by drought (increasingly common in recent years), and waterhole watching becomes an odds-on favorite anywhere and anytime that elk, mule deer, pronghorn, collared peccary (aka javelina) and other western prey are relatively undisturbed. If you're hunting primarily for meat, ambushing at a waterhole can be doubly profitable. While mature bucks and bulls, where hunting pressure is high, may drink only at night, younger males, like females, aren't generally so picky.

Specifically speaking of elk, when I'm hunting areas where water is plentiful – especially if it's running water, which allows animals to drink here one day and a mile downstream the next – I shift my primary focus from water to wallows ... those shallow, generally tub-sized mud holes into which rutting bulls urinate and then roll like horses to cake themselves with their own funky pheromones. Frequently, a bull will bugle while wallowing, or as soon as he's done and before he leaves, helping you locate such midday honey-holes. Approaching a fresh wallow from down-breeze, the stench will often alert you a long way out. Considerations for wallow setups are identical to those for waterholes and other game-attracting natural features: wind, cover, trail locations, sunlight and shade. After years of experimentation, I've come to prefer watching wallows midday, waterholes in the evenings, and sneaking around in silent pursuit of bugling bulls during the morning.

By preparing several ambush setups across a broad area, you can rotate between them and avoid polluting any one place with a cumulative scent trail laid down by your daily comings and goings.

On a typical ambush hunt I spend my active hunting time sitting in deep shade on a stump, fallen log, or just plain dirt (I always carry a small foam butt pad for insulation as well as comfort), leaned semi-comfortably against a tree (but very rarely *in* a tree, unless I'm hunting whitetails), remaining as still as I can manage while doing my best to be ready, moment by moment, for whatever may come my way. Sometimes nothing ever comes. Sometimes it takes forever. Other times it can be an almost continual parade. But any time an animal succumbs to a well-set ambush, the odds are strongly in your favor compared to any other fair-chase hunting strategy.

Ambush: It's traditional. Done right, it's unbeatably effective. By using only natural "baits" like water and natural feeding areas, it's unimpeachably ethical. And by using self-built brush blinds it becomes an economical and satisfying exercise in predatory woodsmanship.

CHAPTER 9

Brushing-in
Building and using natural ground blinds

*These days I hunt from natural cover and am enjoying the time out more
each day. I can move around and explore different areas. It's nice not having
to lug a tree stand and all the items needed for it ... just a fanny pack,
a stool, and my bow. Traveling light and enjoying it.*
                            –Lee Vivian (from a post on *www.tradbow.com*)

Lee Vivian echoes my own passionate preference for traveling light and
unencumbered, and for hunting from natural cover rather than manufactured blinds or tree stands. I rarely (except when hunting whitetails)
perch in a tree, and though I've tried them I don't even own a tent blind.

Yet, fond as I am of brush blinds, I'll stop short of attempting to
argue that natural cover is hands-down the best approach to ambush
hunting for everyone all the time everywhere. As bowhunters with experience across a wide range of game, terrain and cover know well, there
are places where a tree stand or tent blind offers possibly the only stickbow ambush option. What I will say is that walking into the woods (familiar or otherwise), finding a spot that "speaks to me" both strategically and aesthetically, spending a few minutes thoughtfully and minimally
rearranging the vegetation, and then disappearing (like Arnie's *Predator*) into the foliage, has proven to be the most flexible and *enjoyable*
ambush strategy I've found in a lifetime of dedicated ambush hunting.

A piece of camo burlap can turn almost any situation into an impromptu blind.

Check your ambush set-ups for unseen obstructions. (Singeli Eskew)

With natural blinds there's nothing to buy or carry other than a length of twine (for lashing together limbs, etc.) and a couple of small hand tools you likely already own: garden snips for pruning small vegetation, and a compact folding saw for thicker stuff. (Unlike Lee Vivian, I don't even carry a stool, finding an inch-thick, butt-sized foam pad ample for posterior comfort.) No bulky, weighty albatross of metal, plastic and fabric to haul in, put up, take down and eventually haul back out. Nothing to tempt thieves when you're not around, and nothing to replace when it wears out or fails. No safety harness required, and no dark, claustrophobic walls to limit peripheral vision and hearing while restricting shooting opportunities to fixed ports. There's nothing, in sum, to tie you in one place or force you to return to that place (to retrieve gear) when you're done.

Even if you prefer sitting in a tree stand or pop-up blind most of the time, learning to use natural cover is an element of traditional knowledge every serious bowhunter should keep handy in his possibles bag of woodsmanship skills. And the icing on the cake is that while I've never heard anyone call hanging a tree stand or erecting a tent blind "fun," cobbling together an impromptu brush blind *is* fun. Hard to explain why; it just is. Consider ...

Perennial Natural Blinds

Brush blinds have no set configuration or building codes. They needn't even be made of brush. Often, especially on private land, they're substantial affairs built to last, constructed of rocks, logs or earth and trimmed with fresh-cut vegetation. Here in the Rockies, I know bowhunters who have found and hunted successfully from moss-covered stacked-stone waterhole blinds built centuries before by Native hunters. While I haven't been that lucky (and my "friends" aren't sharing their nostalgic finds), I do have a semi-permanent natural blind I've hunted from with good success for some 25 years. And I didn't even have to build it. Rather, this shallow pit-blind built itself when a fat old fir toppled from a steep hillside, ripping out a big root-ball of soil and rocks. The resulting knee-deep crater is about three feet in diameter with a low lump of roots, rocks and dirt in front, a seat-shelf dug into its backside, and situated within longbow range above a well-used spring pool. A few minutes with an E-tool, gardening snips "borrowed" from my wife, and a little folding handsaw, and I had a perennial natural blind that requires mere minutes to refurbish each fall.

Yet the most common, useful and gratifying brush blinds are anything but permanent. In fact, their spontaneous and ephemeral nature is the very essence of their charm. I think of the quickest and easiest such impromptu hides as "rest stops."

Impromptu Natural Blinds

The rest-stop blind is ideal for mobile bowhunters working through big country and can be as informal as a shade tree to lean back against and a stump, log or flat rock (and butt pad, of course) to sit on. Any vegetation trimmed to clear shooting lanes or for bow clearance can be used to enhance the natural cover of the hide. Where most hunters will plop down "wherever" for, say, a brief lunch break, the rest-stop hunter invests a few quiet minutes — seldom more — in converting each of his "rest" stops into slapdash yet functional blinds. After all, the animals are *always* out there and don't necessarily time their movements to accommodate our preferences.

It's easy, and basically the same old ambush story: When possible, select rest stops close downwind from game-concentrating features such as water or food, bedding cover, saddles, scrape lines, or active game trails. After this fashion, in the course of a typical day of relaxed roaming you might (and I often do) cobble together, occupy and abandon several rest-stop hides.

Augmented Natural Blinds

When necessary, don't hesitate to augment a natural hide with cloth "patches," especially if you plan to sit there for any length of time. Early on, one possibility I explored was a camouflaged half-umbrella (the bottom is flat rather than rounded). Available from mail-order hunting suppliers, the half-umby costs and weighs little, rolls into a compact cylinder for easy carrying, and in well under a minute can be opened and placed on the ground or suspended amidst brush, in front or behind you, to supplement natural cover. Even without brush, in ideal conditions a flat-bottomed umbrella can save your bacon when you're walk-and-talk call-hunting, say for turkey or elk, and you get caught off guard and have only moments to make yourself invisible before a responding animal is standing wide-eyed in front of you.

But hunting conditions are rarely ideal, and an umbrella has built-in drawbacks. First, the slick nylon material tends to shine in direct sunlight, a glaring problem that can be largely neutralized by arranging vegetation to break up and partially shade the front surface (if you have time). A more problematic weakness is that an umbrella in the wind is a hang-glider wannabe. Even a light breeze can cause it to shake distractingly, while strong gusts will move it around, pop it inside out, or even kite it away.

That's why I've come to prefer burlap. For less than a buck I can buy used coffee-bean bags from a local caffeine emporium. Such bags are big, originate from all over the world, and come printed with words and various designs, usually in black, that compose an effective camo pattern. Simply cut a coffee bag open, lay it on the grass and give it a good hosing to rinse out the coffee smells, hang it outside for a few days to dry and further deodorize itself, and you're in business. Or, if you prefer, for around $10 at WallyMort you can buy a 10' long by 2' wide bolt of new camouflaged burlap. Cut into two 2'x5' sections (I carry only one at a time), it's all but weightless and yet, when arranged over brush or limbs, remains well behaved even in strong wind. To keep burlap "shed hair" from collecting in my pack during transport (I may carry a burlap panel for days before using it), and to prevent pack contents from transferring game-offending odors to the burlap, I wrap it in a tight bundle tied with twine and strapped to my pack's exterior.

Brushing-in: Ten Tactical Tips

Whether building a long-term natural blind, a temporary rest-stop hide or something in between, the essential strategic considerations remain largely the same:

Locate downwind of where you expect game to appear.

Sit in shade, the darker the better.

Dress in dark colors — many camo patters are far too light (I much prefer dark plaids, especially when leaning back against a tree).

Dig a shallow pit for your boots, or use a slightly elevated seat (stump, log, rock) to enhance comfort and allow sufficient ground clearance to draw and shoot with minimal movement. (A short bow is a tremendous bonus for ambush hunting.)

Substantial background cover is essential to conceal your outline and small movements. A big tree or boulder behind provides a backrest as well as swallowing your head-shoulder silhouette.

While front cover is nice, it's not mandatory if you're dressed to blend in, sitting in deep shade and have good movement control. Generally, front cover should be no more than waist high to facilitate unrestricted drawing, shooting and arrow clearance.

Take care not to spread scent while constructing a blind and clearing shooting lanes. I wear rubber-bottomed boots (L.L. Bean Maine Hunting Shoes) for all mild-weather hunting, and strive to touch surrounding vegetation only with my hand tools, not my hands. All cut vegetation you do touch should be brought back to the blind rather than left scattered around the potential shooting area for animals to happen across.

This fancy brush blind took 15 minutes to build.

Don't totally clear-cut shooting lanes, as alert game may take note of a freshly mowed lawn leading right to you.

Inside your blind, nock an arrow, come to full draw and check for shooting clearance overhead and all around. Trim additional limbs and brush as necessary.

Clear the interior of your blind of ground debris (dry leaves, needles, fallen limbs, small rocks) that could make noise when you stretch or shift positions to shoot.

OK, those are old man Elkheart's bare-bones basics of brushing-in. Refinements are a personal matter and creative fun. And best of all, when the day's hunt is done, you'll have nothing but your trophy to take apart and pack out.

Elkheart's first Coues

CHAPTER 10

The Hardest Hunt of All:

Searching for redemption

Let us begin with a glance back at the timeless sport-hunter's conundrum:

What is a 'trophy'?

Among record book fans, it would certainly not be the little forkhorn Arizona Coues (pronounced to rhyme with "house") whitetail I finally killed after several years of trying. And yet, to take a more thoughtful and aesthetically resonant line of reasoning, the diminutive gray ghost of the Mexican borderlands is among the most difficult of big game animals for fair-chase stickbow hunters to get within range of. Moreover, this desert-adapted whitetail is wound tighter than an armature (and twice as tight when coming to water) and can, on a still morning, hear an arrow sliding slowly over a padded bow shelf from 20 yards and the growl of your stomach from 50. The Coues also has duck-and-spin (aka "string jumping") reactions too fast for a longbow or recurve arrow to outrun, and offers a core kill-zone about the size of a grapefruit. Considering all of this, believe me, *any* Coues killed in fair chase with a stickbow is an *amazing* trophy. So I am appropriately grateful for my first Coues for all these reasons and more. Yet the experience left me haunted by a ghost of regret I just can't banish. Maybe this retelling will help.

As with elk, the hardest part of hunting Coues bucks on public-lands, is finding 'em. Of course, that's the case for most western big game animals scattered across millions of acres of public forest and range lands. With no agriculture or "feed plots" to attract and hold wildlife in places convenient to our ends, public lands hunters are left happily to rely on good old-fashioned scouting: first with e-mail and telephone, then with maps and maybe Google Earth to get ourselves in the ballpark, and finally with boots on the ground to narrow it down and make it real.

And more: Reading informed articles, books and scientific reports (as opposed to Outhouse Channel Hunting Hero hogwash) to educate ourselves about the daily habits and habitats of our intended quarry, is also a smart part of public-lands hunter homework.

That said and even so, it's a *huge* advantage when preparing to hunt an unfamiliar species in unfamiliar terrain to have an experienced friend or two to help you find your way. That's how it was, several years ago now, when fellow traditional bowhunters Greg and John offered to share their considerable combined knowledge of hunting the Sonoran Desert whitetail of southwestern New Mexico and southeastern Arizona. Greg, a retired USFS biologist, lives in the northern Rockies and has been visiting the southern borderlands to chase Coues for weeks at a go every winter for more than a decade. John is a native Sonoran son and retired wildlife manager for Arizona Fish & Game. Both are avid stickbow hunters. (And yes, I'm purposely withholding their last names to protect them from being deluged with unsolicited "Where down there should I go hunting?" emails and calls.)

Prior to Greg inviting me to hunt Coues from his Arizona camp, I'd made just one previous effort, a DIY trip several years before to the

Boot Heel of New Mexico. My companion on that trip was Colorado black bear biologist Tom Beck. An excellent bowhunter is Tom. Yet at that time he knew little more about hunting the almost supernaturally elusive gray desert spooks than I did, his experience being limited to one previous trip when he'd grunted-in a rutting buck that predictably spooked and evaporated. In five days of hard hunting on that virgin New Mexico Coues trip I saw one exceptionally nice, heavy antlered buck, which I roused at under 20 yards from its day bed on a tree-shaded bench while sneak-hunting, plus a couple of does that peered tauntingly down at our canvas tent camp from the safety of a ridge far above. Without elaboration, we two babes in the Coues woods, Tom and I, did a lot wrong, nothing much right and never really had a chance. Still, I love that Geronimo country, recall the adventure with smiles and hope to return someday.

And that was that for about a decade, until Greg invited me to his turf in southeast Arizona a handful of years ago and taught me, primarily through stories from his own experiences, the basics of how it's done. Since then and gradually, through at least two weeks of camping and hunting on my own during each of the next several winters, plus ongoing guidance from Greg and John, I learned the essentials of where to look for Coues and when, and how best to hunt them with stick and string. Even so, a kill continued to elude me. Problem was, finding these covert desert mirages is only the first challenge among many. What I'd yet to learn was how to reach full draw without sound- or motion-spooking the big-eared little rockets, and how to guide an arrow into such a tiny target at max effective range (20 yards for me) when I did get a shot.

The latter problem was and to some extent remains heightened by the fact that for the first time in my life I was hunting from tree stands (not exclusively, but increasingly) and consequently had little experience shooting downward at steep angles. Certainly, I practiced from my cabin's roof at home. Yet, when the pressure was on it became clear that I hadn't practiced enough to offset a lifetime of shooting from the ground and a brain hard-wired to default to that in a pinch. And so it happened, as the hunts came and went and my frustration grew unrequited, that my winter Coues safaris insidiously took on the weight of a personal crusade.

Which brings us to the week before Christmas on a recent Coues hunt. During that intense 12-day solo camp and hunt I got reasonable if not high-odds shots at two pretty bucks, a few days apart, standing relaxed and broadside at about 20 yards. "Clean" misses, both. As I watched, slack-jawed, when the second arrow skittered noisily across the rocky ground and a second taunting white flag disappeared into the oak and manzanita jungle, I was forced to stop and chastise myself ...

"What the heck are you *doing* here, old man, blowing hard-earned shot ops that should be gimmees, and risking wounding an animal in the process?"

Eventually, after an agonizing analysis of why I was missing and with lots of practice from an actual tree stand rather than a roof – and by now, I should point out, the calendar has clicked over from late December to early January and a new year's season (complete with a new $362 nonresident deer tag) – I managed to make a well-placed shot on a fork-horn ... only to watch with aching disbelief as the wood arrow managed less than half-shaft penetration. Had I tumbled from my alligator juniper tree at that moment (that would have to wait another year), it couldn't have been more painful than watching that little buck bound out of sight, my impotent arrow pointing skyward like a scolding finger as he sprinted away, with zero chance he wouldn't die. But when, and where?

And here, at last, we come to the moral meat of this matter, being the unpleasant but essential question: Once we have created every honorable hunter's worst nightmare of lethally wounding an animal yet watching it bound away, what is our moral and ethical duty going forward?

Of course, not all hits that fail to produce a quick death and successful recovery prove fatal to the wounded animal. This is but one of many variables that can coincide to complicate the "What do we owe?" question. Making a good call under such slippery circumstances is always a rough patch for thoughtful hunters, involving deeply personal matters of circumstance, conscience, self-discipline, honor and self-image. But when it comes to predictably lethal hits – one-lungers, gut shots and the like – the clear-cut ethical decision is at once easier ... and far more difficult.

Okay, I'm wandering a bit in my wondering, so let me recap up to now: I finally managed to draw down on a Coues buck at water, just about 20 yards. And I even managed to center an arrow in his chest, broadside. Yet for reasons inexplicable at the time but painfully obvious in the belated light of studied hindsight, the arrow got lousy penetration and the buck took off with half the shaft sticking out — a lurid picture of hunter incompetence that we all want to avoid and on a personal level, makes me want to barf.

After waiting 45 minutes, I de-treed and walked to where the deer had stood when my arrow found him. No blood. The buck had retreated up a wide grassy drainage and I hadn't seen him climb either side before he disappeared around a bend a hundred yards or so west. So off I went on a wholly different kind of hunt, driven by strongly mixed emotions but mostly confidence that such a tiny deer couldn't make it far on just one lung.

Finding no blood along the grassy wash the buck had taken in retreat, and with far too many deer tracks (coming and going to water) to single out a specific set to try and follow, on a hunch I turned up a tight little side cut — and promptly spotted a large pool of fresh red blood on the ground, with more squirted at knee-height on bushes, suggesting an arterial hit. My spirits soared and all worry departed … until I realized that as the buck had continued on, climbing out of the little drainage headed west, his bleeding had abruptly slowed to just a few scattered droplets and even those soon petered out. It's entirely likely that the buck was standing there bleeding when I spooked him with my approach, and had I waited longer to start my search it all might have ended, right then and there, with a successful recovery. Alas, the realities of life and death care naught for second guessing.

Struggling to maintain a hopeful attitude, I spent the next two hours and more in a fruitless search for the animal or its trail. Fortunately, the buck had come to water in late morning so I had an abundance of daylight left and opted to walk back to camp where Caroline and our two dogs were relaxing. With her younger eyes and a pair of untrained but acute canine noses as backups, the search resumed. Over the course of several more hours we collectively, mostly the dogs, found several more tiny specks of blood and successfully extended the trail by a few hundred yards. It was with great reluctance and mounting anxiety that we finally called it a day and returned to camp at sunset, fearful if not yet resigned that the abundant local coyotes would likely win this game.

By a stroke of good luck, we had cell phone coverage on the high ridge where we were camped and I phoned John, pleading my case. My friend, an enviably caring and generous man, readily agreed to be there at daylight the next morning, not a short drive from his home. Far better than merely another pair of eyes, John is a tracker's tracker, having studied this most essential woodsman's craft all his life. Nowadays, in post-retirement, he teaches graduate-level tracking classes to such keenly interested groups as U.S. Marine Corps engineers, who are tasked with the delicate and potentially deadly work of hunting and killing land mines in Afghanistan and elsewhere, without getting killed themselves. If my lost buck could be found, John would find it.

Early on the second morning of this increasingly tense drama, John and I took off provisioned for a long full day's search if necessary. As the hours ticked off and the sun grew hotter I was repeatedly amazed by my friend's tracking skills. While I was focused on trying to spot droplets of blood on the ground, or visible red smears on grass or brush, and finding next to nothing, John's expert eyes repeatedly spotted the tiniest specks of red hiding on the undersides of grass blades or cleverly camouflaged, for example, within the nearly microscopic crenulations of reddish grass seed-heads. Consequently "we" were able to extend the buck's route of retreat another quarter-mile or more by midday. And then, even John hit a wall. Looking back across our route, it became clear that from the point the buck had dropped the big splash of blood the previous day, it had retreated in an almost straight line west, bleeding (externally at least) ever less as it went.

Toward the end, the "trail" had dwindled to a single flea-sized blood dot every several dozen yards, each one requiring excruciatingly patient hands-and-knees inspection to locate. And it was there, standing atop a ridge that tumbled steep downhill to a cottonwood-shaded wash, that the exited croaking of ravens caught our attention. Way down near the bottom, two big black birds circled low above the trees, their obsidian backs glinting in the afternoon sun. We quickly agreed that while John continued his meticulous search to extend the blood trail, I would work down the ridge to see what the ravens were bantering about.

And down there, on the second circle through the brush-choked area, I found my trophy's scant remains: an intact head and neck with death-dulled blue eyes wide open, fronting a mostly naked skeleton. As feared, and utterly predictable in these Sonoran wildlands, coyotes had beat us to it with no inclination for sharing. I took some photos to document the scene of the crime (mine, not the scavengers'), then removed the head from the skeleton and plodded gloomily back up the hill to where John was crawling like a serpent through the grass, still intense in his almost microscopic search for spoor.

And there, with my friend as witness, I somberly punched my pricey nonresident tag and attached it to the diminutive antlers.

The search was over, and so was my Coues hunt for another year.

And we never found the arrow.

Back home in snow-packed mid-winter Colorado, I grew increasingly confident that the dismal penetration that had precipitated the heartbreaking loss of my first, hard-won Coues buck, owed in largest part to a failure to come to full draw in the critical, adrenaline-drunken moment of excitement.

That woebegone shot had been taken, I reminded myself, following repeated episodes of getting busted after making such seemingly inaudible sounds as the muffled squeak of a leather-palmed glove tightening against a leather bow grip, or the equally hushed brush of fletching against beard approaching full-draw. It's likely, in retrospect, that I'd become sufficiently rattled after several such incidents that I likely released prematurely without realizing it, buzzing like a bee on a heavy hit of adrenaline.

Good old target panic.

A likely additive culprit was my weird decision to use a large three-blade broadhead, usually reserved for turkeys only, rather than my usual slender single-bevel two-blade. So many folks swear by three-blades for deer that I'd come to feel I owed them, and myself, a refresher course;

The wages of poor penetration: only the coyotes won.

the last deer I'd killed with a three-blade was my first deer ever, back in 1964. I'd learned long ago to never use a three-blade for elk, after experiencing too many failures to get good penetration even with "perfect arrow placement" with mid-60-pound recurves in my early days of elking. Yet I never doubted that a sharp three-blade on a heavy arrow launched from a 53-pound deflex-reflex longbow would be up to passing through a mini-deer whose chest cavity was only maybe a foot through side to side. While likely a minor problem compared to short-drawing, the added penetration resistance of a big multi-blade couldn't possibly have helped and likely made the disastrous difference.

Whether I'm right or wrong in these postmortem causative conclusions, one positive outcome of the experience was that I determined henceforth to shoot the selfsame arrow set-ups for deer that I use, year after year, with reliable pass-through success on elk. Why risk it ever again? After all, I had in fact gotten "perfect arrow placement," and yet failed to accomplish the most basic moral requirement of any ethical hunter: to recover the game while its flesh is still edible (by me, rather than coyotes). I've also incorporated shooting from high angles into my regular backyard practice routine to improve my confidence in shooting at steep downward angles and thereby lessen stress at the critical moment. And never again, I like to think, will I ever short-draw on game, having practiced locking my shoulders back and getting my right thumb behind my jaw until both have become an integral elements of my "auto-pilot" pre-release check list.

In the end, while I would eagerly call back that wounding arrow if I could, of course I can't. And try as we may (yes, *we*) to the contrary, there likely will be other wounding situations. Consequently, our moral obligation as ethical hunters and humans, in my not-so-humble opinion, is to launch a prolonged, all-out search for seriously wounded game in hopes of finding and tagging whatever may be left, edible or not. In other words, once we screw up a shot, *that* hunt, for the wounded animal, becomes *the* hunt. And finally, we must strive to be as honest with ourselves as possible about the likely causes of any and every shot failure and work diligently to cure those ills in future hunts. The old optimistic cop-out that "Perfect arrow placement is enough," is damn-well *not* enough in every case! To fail, but to learn from the failure experience is personal growth and progress. To fail and learn nothing (Vietnam comes to mind) is stupid, ugly and bodes only ill for the future.

While we can't raise the dead, nor, as Shakespeare's Lady Macbeth was to learn, scrub clean a blood-stained conscience, we can and must do the next best thing: Search long and hard for redemption … in our hearts as well as on the ground.

CHAPTER 11

The Darwin Hunt:

(Mis)adventures of a tree-top flier

I'm seldom seen, especially when I land.

— Stephen Stills, "Tree-top Flier"

Landing — *Whump!* — hard and flat on my back, arms and legs spread-eagle and making involuntary swimming motions, a broken caricature of daVinci's *Vitruvian Man*. I would have chuckled aloud at the brilliant stupidity – in fact, a single misstep – that had gotten me there, if only I could have, but I dared not even try. Panting like a wounded animal, as I swam toward consciousness I heard myself vocalizing every rapid shallow breath with pitiful moans; how embarrassing. Yet I was helpless to stop it. In fact I was quite simply helpless. How many ribs and other bones had I broken? Only one thing was clear at that humbling juncture, and that was pain. Pain in the spine, ribs, low back, right hip, right elbow, left wrist and shoulder, and the back of my head.

"Well," I silently scolded myself, feeling oddly giddy, "just look at the fine mess you've got us into *this* time, old man."

Can't say how long I'd been lying there unconscious, didn't seem long, before my senses clicked back on and my attention was pulled upward to a pair of ravens calling excitedly, circling just above the giant alligator juniper tree from which I'd inadvertently attempted to fly. And

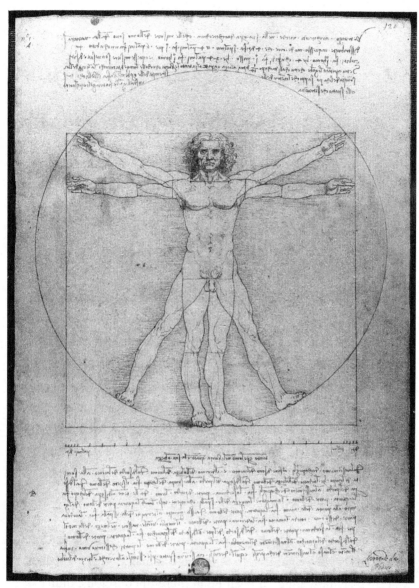

Vitruvian Man

here again I'd have laughed if I dared. Instead, I called back at the ravens via mental telepathy: *"He may be down, but he ain't dead yet!"*

It worked; they went away.

It was New Years Day, opener of archery deer season in southeastern Arizona. I'd rolled into camp early the evening before, oddly untired after a 12-hour drive from Colorado. My first hunt next morning was from a tree stand put up by my local Coues mentor, John, a lifetime southeast Arizonian. Like it or not, stickbow hunting for the hyperspooky Coues, or Sonoran Desert whitetail, is largely a matter of waterhole ambush. Alas, between 7 a.m. and 3 p.m. on opening day – that is, earlier the same day as my fall from sylvan grace – the little cow pond John had set his stand over lured in just one thirsty doe and a sounder of javalinas, for which I had no tag (cost too much and season too short and the meat less than great). Adding to the lack of first-day activity was the further discouraging fact that fresh deer sign around the tank (western-speak for any small body of water) was sparse. Thus, I elected to jump ship and go in search of happier hunting grounds. Coues come to water at midday — an adaptation resulting from having evolved across the past many thousands of years with stealthy mountain lions as their primary predators. So nothing was lost by my leaving in mid-afternoon.

Arriving at a second waterhole a couple of miles south, my enthusiasm was resurrected by an abundance of tiny heart-shaped prints, some not so tiny as others. For the next day or two, I determined, this would be my place. Only one tree stood within longbow range of the water, and it fell far short of perfect. Yet it was that tree or nothing, so I got to work prepping it for a stand. I had the steps in and was clearing small limbs and foliage for a shooting lane before bringing up the stand. The hefty horizontal limb I was standing on was 15 feet up one leg of a V of twin trunks supporting the gnarly, octopus-limbed tree, the gods only know how old.

After finishing the trimming, I tossed down my garden snips and folding saw and turned to step across to the other trunk, where my stand would go — a bit of a stretch but nothing seemingly reckless. But even with my right foot in what felt like solid contact with a stout horizontal branch, as I shifted my balance irretrievably forward the lead foot lost its grip.

Fortunately, with my left hand I had a firm grasp on a sturdy limb projecting at shoulder height from the target trunk.

Unfortunately, when the weight of my falling body slammed home, that "sturdy" limb snapped like a cedar shaft and … *Krack!* … *Whump!*

So there I lay, like I say, a pitiful parody of Leonardo's clockwork *Vitruvian Man*. In fact, landing spread-limbed on my back was a blessing, in that it spread the impact throughout my body. Had I landed standing, it's likely that the focused shock would have driven my femurs into my armpits. And my wife prefers tall guys.

Yet even the exquisite pain had a silver lining, in that it told me I was still alive, conscious, and discounting a few ribs nothing critical seemed obviously broken. Assuming I could stand, or even get to my knees, I figured I could hobble or negotiate the hillside the few hundred steep brushy and rocky yards up and out of the little canyon in whose bottom sat the pond, then another half-mile or so of level cow-pasture hobbling or crawling back to the truck.

Nothing to it, Gramps.

But what if it turned out there *was* something to it?

Only one person in the universe knew where I was, and only in general terms, since I hadn't told John I was shifting ponds. More chilling yet, it would take a couple of days without hearing from me before my wife, back home, would work up enough worry to call and ask John to come looking. And by then, if I couldn't haul myself out of this fine mess on my own, I'd likely be pecked to death by ravens, robbed by illegal space aliens and devoured by coyotes before anyone could find what remained of me.

After half an hour or more lying there, my breathing became a little easier and the volume and frequency of my moans decreased. I could see clearly, no double vision, suggesting that a concussion wasn't likely, notwithstanding my head had landed on a small rock and the flesh wound was soaked with clotting blood. In context to the bigger pains and concerns, all such superficial insults to the flesh, and there were many, hardly even registered.

With great effort and caution I rolled onto one side. So far, so good. Bow and pack lay almost within reach, reassuring. But my right leg, somewhere between excruciating pain and numbness, didn't feel as if it would hold its share of standing weight; the hip, I worried, might be fractured. So rather than try and stand, I wormed my way the short distance to the tree from which I'd just failed to fly and propped myself upright against its reptilian trunk. I coughed and spat up at blood.

And that's when the weirdness kicked in.

My next move was not merely sloppy, as falling from a perfectly good tree had been, but should qualify old Elkheart for at least an Honorable Mention in the annual Darwin Awards "too dumb to live" competition. To be a serious competitor for top-10 Darwinian honors, one has to commit accidental suicide by crass stupidity, which I intended if possible to avoid henceforth. Problem was, the old cowboy "wisdom" advising fallen heroes to "Git rat back on the horse what throwed ya" or else be afraid of horses forever henceforth had popped into my rattled head and stuck there like bad song lyrics. And too, I had once been a Marine and for those who may not know, the second part of the name "Marine Corps" is there for a very good reason: "Do or die." But this was no war, except within myself, and my better judgment was easily defeated when suddenly, illogically, perhaps insanely, getting back up that tree became even more important than getting back to camp; like, "If I can do *this*, I can handle anything."

And so it was, giving in to the cowboy bumper-sticker fool's dare – "Are you going to cowboy up, or just lay there and bleed?" – I used the lower tree steps to pull myself to my feet. Applying light weight to my right leg I found it painfully lacking, as expected. And so, with one functional leg and two aching but operable arms I lugged my crippled bod, so recently unconscious, back up and into the saddle of the "horse what throwed me." After securing myself to the main trunk with a safety line at the 20-foot level, I pulled the stand up and fastened it in place.

Back on the ground (having arrived there upright this time), feeling triumphantly stupid but triumphant still, I rested a few minutes before collecting my pack and bow, cutting a sturdy manzanita branch for a staff, and lurching in fits and starts up the hill. From the top, with the whole bizarre scene of the previous few hours now dramatized by a flaming desert sunset, I used a barbed-wire fence as a limp-along lifeline back to camp.

"Camp" in this case was a truck camper parked along a dirt back road used only (except in hunting season) by the occasional rancher or Border Patrol vehicle. While cell phones have no place in hunting, in order to get my wife's blessing for this 12-day solo excursion, I had one in the truck. The person I needed to talk to just then wasn't Caroline, but Doc Dave Sigurslid, hunting bud and fellow recreational campfire philosopher. After guiding me through a series of mobility tests, my personal physician allowed as how I "probably" didn't have any broken bones, including the dysfunctional hip. "Take a day or two off," he advised. "Use a walking stick and take slow short hikes on easy terrain. Do some gentle stretches. Try to pull your bow and see how far you get. Don't push too hard. Let pain be your guide. Take three ibuprofen three times a day, a shot of bourbon every night before bed, and keep in touch. Tough it out, Marine!"

Good advice as always from Doktor Dave. And sure enough, by the second morning after the fall I could pull my 53-pound longbow to almost full draw and optimistically assumed adrenaline would finish the job should I get a shot opportunity. And increasingly, I was limping around without support.

Typical Arizona Coues country

Elkheart's 4x5 Darwin Hunt Coues

Back to the hunt!

Across the rest of the week I alternated between perching in what I'd dubbed the Darwin Tree, and John's stand down the way. And in both places I saw only does. Where were the rutty bad boys? Why weren't they chasing the girls?

Aside from the fall, an annoying issue throughout this hunt was that a baiter (as opposed to a hunter) had appropriated my favorite Coues pond, where I'd profitably hunted from a safely grounded brush blind in previous years and the only place I'd found where wind patterns would allow that luxury. Incomprehensibly, Arizona allows the baiting of deer and our resident baiter – a shade-tree outfitter hired by a big city client – was working it to the max. In addition to hauling in a bale of alfalfa and a bucketful of "sweet feed" every Friday evening preparatory to his clients' weekend "hunts," Bubba Baiter had placed several game cameras around the area and a tree stand some 35 yards from the bait (compound shooter). From my point of view, the precise little piece of Arizona that I drove 568 one-way miles to enjoy had been poisoned and rendered useless, unfairly denying me access to public land. Granted, my ground blind was on the opposite side of the pond and blocked by the earthen dam from view of the bait. Yet if I were to try and ignore the bait and kill a buck there, I would feel I had killed a baited deer. And to one degree or another I would have. Thus, I found myself unjustly dispossessed and relegated to more remote, less productive waters.

Withal, between my near-death tumble and the amateur interference of a couple of clueless losers, my prospects for a successful or even enjoyable hunt weren't exactly budding, and the days were clicking by.

Then, with only two hunting days left before I had to head home, brother John took pity and directed me to one of his "super-secret personal honey holes."

And such a place it was! Not only had every minute spent in the Darwin Tree tormented me with painfully embarrassing memories of the fall, the trunk and thus the stand were pitched forward and damned uncomfortable. By comparison, this new Secret Tree was refreshingly friendly. Another alligator juniper, it offered a secure and comfortable perch just 12 feet up, measured at butt height. Better yet, lush evergreen boughs curved forward like hairy arms on either side to hide my silhouette and keep me in shade through most of the day.

After relocating my stand late the same day I pulled it from the Darwin Tree, I made camp a half-mile away, on the far side of a timbered hill. There, I enjoyed a luxury dinner of salad, bread and homemade elk green chili stew, capped by a bourbon-assisted (doctor's orders!) 12 hours' healing sleep. Early the next morning I was sipping thermos coffee in the Secret Tree, feeling like a new old man. While everything about me still ached, in this fresh-start place I felt a sense of renewed hope and energy. And attitude, you know, is everything.

Even so, the morning started slowly, with only scrub jays coming to water and the mindless mooing of Arizona longhorns in the distance, conveniently separated from my "water" by a fence. It wasn't until mid-morning that I heard a tiny *Tink!* somewhere behind me and turned to see a Coues doe sailing gracefully over that fence. Within moments the welcome arrival was joined by a second doe and the pair, after a good look-around, started feeding cautiously my way. While I wasn't hunting does, I was nonetheless excited to have these "test deer" to entertain me and warm up on. Ever on the razor's edge of panicked flight, which is the species' wont, the two prudent girls took half an hour to feed some 40 yards to the water, then another 10 minutes in drinking, politely taking turns so that at least one slender long neck was always stretched upright, senses on hyper alert. Yet I felt confident I could have killed either doe from my most excellent new stand. Better yet, they had approached from downwind and never caught my scent, confirming my sense that the warming midday air was gently rising.

It was straight up noon and the does were long gone when the 4x5 appeared. Unlike the flighty does, this obviously rutty fellow almost ran to water, stopping only once en route to glance around. When he lowered his head to drink and it didn't pop right back up again to catch any approaching danger by surprise, as so often happens with elk and especially pronghorn, I saw no reason to delay, came effortlessly to full draw (good ole' adrenaline), and the arrow zipped away.

Just 15 yards out and 12 feet up — for an experienced tree-stander, it was candy. For me, having only recently taken up tree standing, and only for whitetails, I was still struggling to internalize holding low for steep-angled shots and ... well, I shot high. Though well forward as it should be, my arrow smacked audibly into the animal's spine before turning sharply (I assumed and would later confirm a ricochet) down through the off-side lung. The bushwhacked buck went down like a dropped brick, hind-end paralyzed but front legs frantically paddling the air and ground, seeking traction and escape.

"Oh God," I moaned aloud, *"not this, please."* I *hate* spine shots and would never intentionally take one. If I could have, I would have called that arrow back and walked away in gratitude. Mercifully for all concerned, before I could string another arrow for a follow-up shot, a spray of blood erupted from the buck's nostrils and mouth and his struggling ceased. While it had lasted only seconds, it felt like forever to me.

Back on the ground I approached my unmoving prey. Shaken as I was, in need of absolute, even redundant confirmation of death, I knelt and from 10 yards took a precisely placed insurance shot. This arrow got it right, cutting a huge "tear" entry wound just behind the ribs then angling forward through both lungs to slice off a thin edge of off-side scapula. Only the ground stopped the heavy-fronted arrow's further progress.

With the buck now double-dead and the warming desert day at full sun, I dragged my miniature trophy a few yards into the shade and prepared for the bloody work. And bloody it was. In addition to the copious blood that had blown from nostrils and mouth, the body cavity was a tub of blood and the internal organs evidenced the signature "homogenization" I've come to expect from a scalpel-sharp single-bevel broadhead literally screwing its way through soft tissue. Before skinning, I tried with mixed results for some images of the buck's head and mine, with my camera held at arm's length. (I couldn't get the time delay to work, depriving me of properly composed hero shots.) Pretty much failing in that, I put away the uncooperative camera and used a Swiss Army knife (having sleepily left my belt knife back in camp) to skin and quarter the approximately hundred-pound (live) animal. Being accustomed to dealing with elk, the work went remarkably fast even with gimpy arms and a wimpy knife. And when it was done, all the meat fit easily into a single elk-quarter game bag. The graceful head and delicate antlers were destined for a skull-plate mount, hair on, which now resides in my living room. It was my nicest Coues to date.

As so often is the case with ambush hunting, especially from a tree stand, the fleeting moments defining the actual kill, while exciting, are downright routine compared to the days of challenge and effort and mystery and uncertainty and occasional hardship that bring us to that poignant apogee.

For embarrassingly obvious reasons, I've christened this rags-to-riches adventure the "Darwin Hunt," which I'm deeply grateful concluded upright, rather than flat on my back on opening day, beneath the Darwin Tree.

Postscript: Back home, Caroline noted my jake-leg limp and asked about it. To save her worry, I hadn't told my wife anything from Arizona other than "I'm a bit sore tonight; took a little fall." But now, fessing-up in full, I pulled up my shirt and dropped my drawers to reveal a coal-black bruise a foot wide and more than twice that long angling across my lower back and right hip. My right forearm and bicep were likewise solid black and blue. After gasping aloud at the morbid sight, my wife asked (rather indelicately, I thought): "That must have really hurt. Did you cry?"

"No," I replied, "not then. A few days later, when I shot the deer, then my eyes got wet." I did not tell her why.

Post-postscript: After hearing through the hunters' grapevine that the Arizona Wildlife Commission was considering a ban on deer baiting, I sent a polite but firm letter to those folks explaining how unfair it was to fair-chase hunters, not to mention unethical and a disease risk for the animals, and expressed my reluctance to continue my cherished habit of spending at least two weeks and a thousand bucks down there every winter, unless and until baiting, at least over water, was outlawed. After sending the email to Arizona I copied it to every traditional bowman I knew who hunted down there, asking that they also write and demand an end to baiting. And they did. And the commission did in fact outlaw deer baiting, starting in January of 2014. While I doubt a handful of outraged nonresident hunters were the primary force for good in this event, I can't imagine that our letters and phone calls did the cause any harm.

Yes, we are insignificant individuals. Yet, sometimes the magic works ... but only if we give it a try. It's the American way. Use it or lose it.

CHAPTER 12

A Spring Turkey Tip-sheet

Let's take a break for a bit from talk of hunting hooved animals and turn for a few pages to America's only "big game" bird, the wild turkey. While I'll be specifically addressing hunting the Merriam's subspecies in mountainous terrain, as it's commonly done in the West and the only kind of turkey chasing I know enough about to talk about, any necessary regional differences in tactics have more to do with the terrain than with the birds themselves. Turkeys are, after all, birds of a feather.

Wild turkey toms, like traditional bowhunters, are fiercely individual and often just as fiercely eccentric. Consequently, there is no one strategy or set of strategies to guarantee success in bowhunting for them. There are, however, some essential *constants* of spring turkey bowhunting, the most important of which are reviewed here — along with a flock of more advanced "in the trenches" tactics that I find handy.

Scouting

A week or two (or three) before opening day, don your camo (why advertise?) and go ghosting through known turkey habitat searching for fresh sign: glimpses of the birds themselves; big green-white droppings (crudely J-shaped tubes are tom, while pies and plump straight tubes are hen); the black, tarry, malodorous excretions of the cecum (sniff it and you'll wish you hadn't); feeding scratches (often but not always fan-shaped) in ground litter; dusting areas; dropped feathers; tracks (tom prints can be up to half again larger than hen tracks and, unlike hens, the middle toe is significantly longer than the outside two); and roost trees. The latter will have sturdy, open, near-level lower limbs, with a profusion of feathers and droppings decorating the ground below. Ponderosa pines along ridges and riparian cottonwoods are much preferred nocturnal perches.

Get into the woods a bit before first light, sit or walk quietly and listen for gobbles, hen talk and fly-down wing beats. If the toms aren't vocalizing, call loudly with a crow, owl, coyote yipper or other "locator" call to elicit shock gobbles. (Please don't use a turkey call pre-season unless you prefer hunting educated birds.) As soon as you've gathered the intelligence you need, withdraw quietly and stay away until the evening before the season opening, when you may want to creep back in to the edge of your planned hunting area and do some locator calling at or just after dusk — a ritual known as "roosting your bird."

When calling to ...

A roosted gobbler: In full darkness, approach a roosted and gobbling tom generally no closer than a hundred yards, set up — when possible, to the west of the roost tree, since morning birds prefer to feed with the sun to their backs; or, if your scouting has identified an active feeding area nearby, set up between it and the roost. At the first hint of dawn, scratch out two or three quiet, calm clucks or yelps — the pre-fly-down tree call of the hen. Don't overdo it. If a roosted tom gobbles back immediately, he has acknowledged your presence and location; call no more until you hear him fly down, then imitate a hen's fly-down cackle—a series of several rapid, curt yelps followed by a few standard yelps. At the same time you're cackling, imitate fly-down wing beats by slapping your cap against your leg a few times at half-second intervals (easier to manage, of course, of you're using a mouth-held diaphragm call, which all solo turkey bowhunters should learn to master in any event). Since undisturbed wild turkeys frequently use the same roost trees night after night unless badly disturbed (true especially for the Merriam's and Rio Grande subspecies), never risk spooking a tom on or near his roost. If things don't work out, slip quietly away and return to try another morning.

A gobbler on the ground: If a tom comes off the roost and doesn't head immediately your way, offer him a mix of yelps, feeding purrs and cuts — the latter being a series of a dozen or so loud, sharp clucks; fewer could be taken by the tom as alarm putts. (Cutts are made by hard-tapping the striker rapidly on a slate or glass call, rapping the paddle briskly on the edge of a box call or using the tip of your tongue to make rapid *tutt-tutts* on a diaphragm; be sure to practice first, modeling your sound after real hens you hear in the woods.) Let the tom set the calling pace. If he's gobbling frequently and aggressively, yelp likewise. If he's frugal with his gobbles, be equally stingy. And either way, be patient.

If a recently off-roosted tom gobbles to your calling but moves away rather than toward you, he's most likely with hens and headed for a feeding/breeding area. Quit calling, drop quietly back away from the bird and circle wide and fast until you're well ahead along the flock's projected path, then set up, wait for the gobbler to approach within a hundred yards or so and resume calling.

As long as you can keep a gobbler talking within earshot, you have a chance at him. If a tom comes off the roost and moves promptly out of hearing range or clams up, quietly withdraw and hunt elsewhere, then return to the roost area just before noon and try again; a spring tom will often check back at home base during late morning through midday, especially if more pressing commitments to hens awaiting him on the ground forced him to ignore a flirty hen (you) yelping there at daylight.

Early-season, "fresh" birds: If fly-down time passes and you're not yet on a talking bird, walk slowly and quietly, keeping to the shadows, and cluck and yelp often and loud — or use a locator call — until you elicit a response gobble. It might take seconds or it might take hours. Or it might not come at all that day. Still, it's the best bet at such times. If subsequent gobbles suggest a bird is coming to you, set up immediately. This can be made easier and more productive if you call from locations where you've identified a potentially lucrative set-up. Some experienced turkey bowhunters, having been busted by charging toms, I and I included, *never* call unless we are at least peremptorily set up. If a bird responds but doesn't come, move in as close as you dare — keeping in mind that toms like open approach lanes with no obstructions that would prevent them from displaying — then set up and resume calling.

Late-season, call-shy toms: If you know turkeys are around but they're not sounding off, call sparingly, relying more on locator calls and calm clucks and purrs than the more urgent yelps and cutts. Patience is paramount. Find a good set-up in a likely spot (more about which in a moment) and call once every 15 minutes or so for at least an hour, keeping alert for the sneaky approach of a silent bird. (Listen for the *Pop!* and *Whoof!* sounds of tail fan spreading and wings opening in display, and for sometimes surprisingly loud footsteps in the forest duff.) If luck evades you, move quietly on to a fresh set-up and repeat the drill. In my experience, short of turkey wing-bone "suckers," which very few hunters ever learn to master (again, including I and I), slate calls make the most realistic turkey sounds and often work best with tongue-tied toms. But not always. To cover all bets I carry a slate, a box and an assortment of diaphragms, using a different call each time I sound off until I find the one that elicits a response from the particular tom I'm working. Every tom seems to prefer a slightly different sound, even as those individual preferences can shift inexplicably from moment to moment. If the local birds won't talk turkey no matter what, use locator calls to try and prompt shock gobbles as you're searching for a new set-up.

Hang-ups: Most often, a tom that gobbles and comes part-way in, then stops (hangs up), is either with hens or has encountered a ground obstacle such as a stream, gully, big downed log or fence row. If you can hear hens with the tom, call aggressively with loud, raspy cutts spiced with clucks and yelps, imitating the dominant-sounding hen in the approaching flock. Upstage her, cutting her calls off with your own; be rude. This may pull her in for a showdown — with the tom close in tow.

No hen talk? Then a ground obstacle may be the problem. Try switching calls and vary your calling style. If your boy starts moving away, switch calls again and slow the cadence. Toss in a few calming purrs and use your fingers or a stick to scratch in the ground litter (patterns of three quick scratches, pause, three quick scratches, work well for me).

In either event, whether hens or a physical obstacle in the woods, if you're hunting with a partner, double up on your combined calling to imitate a flock. If solo, call with a diaphragm and box or slate simultaneously. Or purr while scratching the ground and slapping your trousers with your cap to emulate two toms scrapping — often a profitable caper for un-sticking a stubborn tom.

If you're stuck bird comes unglued in the wrong direction and begins moving off (or falls silent, which often but not always means he's moving away), it's time to stretch your legs. Quietly stand and, taking advantage of available cover and shadows, move quietly away from the tom, pausing to yelp every 50 yards or so. When you've backed up a couple hundred yards, call one last time then quickly and quietly retrace your retreat route back toward the tom; set up again but call no more. Often, if a hung-up tom hears a yelping hen moving away, he'll abandon his trepidations and follow after silently ... and you'll be waiting in ambush along his approach route. If you're hunting with a partner, retreat together, yelping as you go, with one of you going full back while calling, the other ceasing to call and stopping 50 yards ahead to set up. (If this sounds reminiscent of the way two hunters might work a rutting bull, it's because the tactics are identical.)

Another good bet for a hung-up, silent and/or retreating tom is to quit calling, drop quietly back then circle wide and fast around the reluctant bird, then set up and call again from the opposite side. Thank the hunting goddess that turkeys have no sense of smell!

As a desperate last resort, gobbling to a hung-up tom may bring him in when nothing else will — but never gobble unless you are *positive* there are no other hunters (especially the itchy-fingered shotgun variety) within hearing.

A gobbler within sight: Your first glimpse of an approaching tom is likely to be his bobbing white-capped skinhead. No matter how furiously he's yakking as he comes in, tone your own calling way down as the heat increases, calling quietly and just often enough to keep him hot (some veterans stop calling entirely). Be aware that any turkey you've called in will have your precise location fixed before strutting into sight. Don't even blink if he's in sight, and that's no mere cliché. If he folds his tail and periscopes his neck, he's looking for that horny hen who invited him in. Now is when your set-up and sixth sense for timing will make or break your hunt.

Set-up

In bowhunting for wild turkeys, more so than for any other game animal I know, set-up is everything. Like most successfully evolved prey species these big birds are survival specialists. Their bulging, side-set eyes constantly scan for danger in all directions. (I've had approaching toms spot my camouflaged form through brush so thick I couldn't see them at all.) Spotting any fast movement is their cue to putt and run. Their hearing is uncanny — superior, in my experience, to any wild ungulate except perhaps the Coues whitetail. If turkeys had a sense of smell, killing one with a stickbow would be all but impossible. In sum, while turkeys are dumb as doorknobs in human terms, their jittery fear of almost everything, combined with lightning instincts, make them geniuses in their own wild world — which is why they're so prolific and so very much fun to hunt, win or lose.

As I've said, I prefer to set up before calling; you never know when a tom is nearby and may come galloping in at remarkable speed. A spring gobbler likes to strut in to a calling hen—tail fanned wide, wings half-extended and held low so that the tips drag the ground, stepping with a haughty, head-bobbing gait. To accommodate this flashy showmanship, he needs a fairly open approach avenue: a closed logging road with the grass grown over, a power-line trail, a wide game path or finger meadow. When he gets to where he thinks the calling hen can see him, he'll want a spacious stage on which to perform his pow-wow dance. Thus, the most effective set-up is at the edge of a small clearing with an open approach lane leading into the clearing from the singing gobbler's direction. Never set up in dense woods or brush that could obstruct shot lanes or present obstacles to a fickle tom's approach, and remember that it's usually easier to call a tom uphill or across level ground than to lure him downhill.

Arrowing a wild spring turkey with a traditional longbow or recurve is one of the most difficult challenges in the hunting world; in my experience, the turkey challenge is equaled only by attempting to stalk a pronghorn or Coues whitetail. It's some easier for two archers working together. As in hunting bull elk in rut, the shooter sets up 20 to 50 yards out front of the caller, along the quarry's expected approach lane—but it's still no turkey shoot. Since you'll almost certainly be shooting from a sitting or kneeling position, conduct your practice sessions accordingly. Camo your bow as well as yourself and avoid bright-colored fletching, especially red, white or blue, a wad of which projecting from a quiver could not only spook a colors-conscious turkey but also get you shot by another hunter. I've even had the glint of a stainless broadhead tip a tom to trouble and send him running. (I like big, multi-blade heads like the Snuffer for turkeys, usually with a penetration limiter, and I paint the whole works flat black.) Since the only chance you'll have to draw undetected on an approaching tom is when his back is turned and his tail fanned, or his head is hidden behind a tree, set up with scattered trees to your front and open shooting lanes between.

Decoys

"Dekes" are both a godsend and a curse for bowhunters. My favorite decoy set-up — in fact, the only set-up I know that consistently works with the mountain Merriam's I mostly hunt — requires one or two hen and one jake decoy and a large tree near the center of a small clearing, 10 or 15 yards to the front of your deep-shaded hiding spot. Place the hen/s a few yards on the opposite side of the tree, hidden from your view. Place the jake on your side of the tree and facing you. (If it's windy, mount the jake low to the ground with rocks or sticks on either side of the tail to keep it from swinging around away from you.) Always try to have all decoys fully exposed to the sun for highest visibility.

When a tom approaches — and when the magic is working — he'll spot the fake tarts, hit full strut and, predictably, do one of three things: A mature, confident tom will generally head straight for the fake jake, face the dummy head-on and display, in the process blocking his view to the back with his fanned tail, enabling you to draw and shoot, aiming for the anal vent. Or, the tom may ignore the jake and head for the hen/s, circling like a band of Hollywood Indians harassing a wagon train. When his head is behind that strategically chosen tree, come to full draw and you'll be set to take the shot when he steps clear moments later.

A third possibility, of course, is that an approaching tom — which will be expecting the hens not only to move but to come to him—will become suspicious of the hens' inaction, hang up just out of range or sight, pace and putt for a moment, then take a powder. Since I much prefer to kill jakes (they're tender enough to actually taste good) and have learned that jakes often run away at first sight of a jake decoy, I use only the hen if I know it's a jake coming in. Although jakes will sometimes gobble, especially when they're in a bachelor group of several birds, most often they merely yelp. But it doesn't take long to learn to distinguish between the loud, coarse, persistent yelps of an approaching jake and those of a hen.

Another lucrative decoy ploy for bowhunters is to set out your fake(s) along a linear strutting lane — closed logging roads are perfect — and 10 to 20 yards beyond your hide, opposite the direction from which you expect your bird to approach. As your tom nears, turn your head away to throw your yelps away from him, beyond you and toward the decoys. Quit calling as the gobbler closes and make like a marble statue as he passes. If the mojo is working, he'll spot the dekes and display. Draw and shoot only when his tail is fanned and his head hidden.

A final decoy note: In my experience, toms will often approach a fake hen or jake aggressively, stop and take a quick look from as far out as 20 yards, sense a rat in the woodwork (you) and exit pronto. So take the first sure shot opportunity.

Or better yet, at least when hunting birds in the forest, don't use decoys at all. I've easily lost more toms to "decoy panic" on their part, or getting caught by a fast-approaching tom while I hurriedly setting out dekes, than I've ever lured into longbow range. A fair compromise is to put out a decoy only when the wind is blowing sufficiently to lend it some movement and verisimilitude to life. A deke that just sits there unmoving while a tom does his best to get it sexually excited, is almost certain to find prompt rejection. Hunting the eastern subspecies at the edges of crop fields from a portable blind using big spreads of decoys is utterly beyond my experience and thus beyond my right to comment on, but would seem to be productive, if not very exciting.

Elkheart with fall jake

Jake track

Aiming points

On a broadside bird, aim high and forward, approximately at the junction of wing and body (wing butt). Unlikely as it sounds (it took me *years* to figure this out, apparently learning nothing by sticking my fist inside to pull the innards out), that's where the vitals on a turkey are located ... as opposed to forward and *low* for most mammals. With a front-on tom, focus on the beard attachment, though it's highly unlikely (unless you're in a tent blind) that you can draw and get an accurate shot off from that angle without being busted. From behind the bird, shoot for the natural bulls-eye at the center of the tail if fanned (that is, the bung hole), or aim mid-back on a tail-folded bird — a spine hit is the *best possible* body shot on a turkey. Use a large, sharp broadhead and, if you're shooting a heavy bow, a penetration limiter. Though I haven't heard much about them in a while and they were never popular for bowhunting Merriam's in the Rockies, it makes sense that in the right circumstances "string trackers" can notably increase your chances of re-covering wounded hidden birds.

Weather

Rain: A mild drizzle or brief shower has little effect on the routine activities of wild turkeys; keep your calls dry and hunt as usual. Serious rain, when the trees and underbrush are dripping and making a disori-enting amount of noise, sends turkeys into open areas such as closed roads, forest clearings, pastures and fields, where they can see approach-ing predators the rain could prevent them from hearing; look for them there. A prolonged hard rain puts turkeys on the roost, and you might as well head home as well.

Wind: Like light rain, strong wind makes wild turkeys nervous and supremely cautious, as it does deer and other big game. Another, per-haps even more daunting problem with wind and turkeys is that un-less you're in one another's laps, the birds can't hear you and you can't hear them. Use your loudest call and listen carefully for responses. If the wind is uneven, call during breaks between gusts. Often, turkeys will flock to open areas on windy (as with rainy) days so that they can see, if not hear, approaching danger, thereby escaping the potentially fatal visual distractions of windblown and constantly moving vegetation. Conversely, since a strong wind can actually blow a displaying tom smack over on his pretty face (yes, I've seen it), they'll often retreat to wind-sheltered cover, such as gully-bottoms, the lee sides of hills and dense woods. Look for them there.

After the shot

Forget the standard archery deer hunter's waiting game rule and get right on a wounded turkey. Gather up your gear and walk (don't run) to the bird. A wounded tom that's able to fly or run will often retreat in a fairly straight line. Watch him as long as you can, then search along a line from your set-up to where you last saw the bird ... and as far beyond as necessary. While it's rare to find anything resembling a blood trail, a few scattered feathers and tracks may help to mark the way.

Usually within a few hundred yards at most, a seriously wounded turkey, whether he flew or ran away, will go to ground, often tunneling back into thick brush or weaseling up under a tangle of roots. There, he'll fold his wings, pull his head down into his breast feathers and lie still as a stone while you walk by only steps away. Search all such likely hiding areas carefully, looking for a dark mass, specks of color and especially (just like rabbit hunting) a big shiny black eye. If your arrow stays in the bird it will complicate his flying, running and hiding — thus my preference for big heads and penetration limiters. The best of all possible arrow shots on a turkey is when he's positioned with an ample tree, a dirt bank or another impenetrable backstop close behind to prevent the arrow from passing completely through the bird while pinning him to the backstop like a butterfly to a collection board.

Safety

I've already spoken of the importance of avoiding wearing or carrying American-flag colors in the turkey woods. If you hunt with a partner, always know his or her exact whereabouts before you shoot. (I have a personal near-miss story that still makes me shudder to recall; to the point I can't bear to repeat it here.) Never shoot except at a visible turkey with a visible beard. Never attempt to stalk in on a calling hen or gobbler; you'll either spook the bird or, if it's the wrong species of turkey, he just might blow your lips off with a 12-bore.

Summary

This conglomeration of turkey tips, while based in my personal experience with Merriam's in the mountains, nonetheless fairly cover most of what you'll likely encounter in the spring woods, no matter where you live or hunt (with the popular exception of hunting over crops, which requires no woodsmanship whatsoever but only a tent blind, a wad of dekes and a call). Still, nobody's saying that killing a gobbler with a stickbow will be anything short of real damned hard. That's what makes it so much fun and worth all the early morning risings.

Bears, like people, must eat to survive and support their families.
It's people, not bears, who are the problem.

CHAPTER 13

Adventures with Blackie
The true trash on "garbage" bears

As usual during this most magical of seasons, I'm haunting an aspen grove not far from home, hoping for elk and adventure. Just now, I'm listening to a big bull bugling from a quarter-mile away, maybe farther, attempting to visualize his travel route so that I can circle ahead to intercept him ... when suddenly a bear appears, big as life and black as any cave. The outsized head and feet, lanky legs and other clues suggest an underfed and (it follows logically) hungry animal.

And no wonder. Freaky weather — a drought winter combined with late-spring frosts — has thrown the local ecology woefully out of whack, rendering natural bear chow scarce. No chokecherries or service berries. No acorns. Even the grasses, sedges, forbs and deciduous leaves are drying and dying weeks early. Consequently, these woods are crawling with starving bruins, reduced to eating ants. And down in the valleys, where the humans live, every trash can has its own private bear.

Nor can you blame the bears. Ursids prefer wilderness habitat and wild foods. But wildness has failed them this year, exacerbated by the tragic fact that humans now occupy much of the best wildlife habitat: riparian greenways and valley meadows. Besides, no bear can raid a garbage can that isn't left out, or invade a bear-proofed dumpster. Nor will it be motivated to rip into your tent in the middle of the night if there's nothing in there, including you, that smells like food. Rather than "bad animals," most "problem" bears I've known (and I've known a few) are victims of natural circumstance and the willful ignorance of careless humans.

Ignoring me, the bear in front of me now — guess I'll just call him Blackie, since black-colored "black" bears are a rarity here in the southern Rockies — briefly sniffs the ground, then flops down and rolls joyously, like a just-unsaddled horse. Done with that, he stands, shakes like a wet dog and sits, just fifteen yards away. As he gazes bemusedly toward the distant bugling bull, it strikes me that he too must be hunting elk, with a strategy that mirrors my own.

Soon enough and inevitably, the breeze wanders, the best nose in the woods catches my whiff and Blackie stands to check me out, his big head weaving and bobbing, nostrils twitching.

Wanting no confusion or trouble, I stand too, wave my arms and quietly say, "Go away, bear. I was here first."

But the bear doesn't move.

OK. I shake my bow menacingly and do a little war dance, trying to look mean.

Blackie only stares, perceiving the benign reality behind my fearsome guise. And it's true: For me, among the greatest pleasures of sneaking around in camouflage, bowhunting for elk, is meeting lots of bears, up close and personal. I could never kill one. For starters, though I've eaten it and can't say it's bad, I have no stomach for bear meat, and the first test of ethical hunting, in my book, is to kill only what you really want to eat. Above and beyond that, throughout human history, bears have been perceived as special, even magical beings — shadows of our primal selves. I feel this magic strongly, and so I don't hunt bears.

To the contrary, I see myself as an ursid benefactor. Should I find the luck to kill an elk this year (as I do most every autumn), Blackie or another of his hungry tribe will benefit magnanimously from the viscera, bone marrow, meat scraps and whatever else can be salvaged from the birds and bugs. It's an ancient, traditional and utterly appropriate hunter's tithe to wildness. And in lean years such as this, just one elk gut pile is a windfall that could provide enough calories to see a lean bear through the long dark denning months ahead.

Yet, for his own good, this fearless fellow needs a shot of aversive conditioning. So I place a rubber-tipped grouse arrow on my bowstring and aim for the big black butt. But before I can let the stinger fly, Blackie, apparently taking the clue, suddenly wheels and shuffles away — if only a few yards — then haunch-sits again and resumes his staring. I hold my shot ... and moments later, when the momentarily forgotten wapiti bugles again, I remember what I'm here for and slowly back away.

Blackie just sits and watches me go.

As so often happens when I try to approach an evening-bugling bull, he sings no more and in the end I walk home, meatless and in the dark, thinking bearish thoughts.

Come morning, I decide to weasel into the local elk bedding area early, from whence the bull was bugling last evening, while the big deer are still out and about on their morning feed and carouse. Surprise them when they return. Toward that end, I'm following a freshly churned elk path as it drops down to cross a brushy draw, when I feel my skin prickle with that ancient sixth-sense awareness — you just *know* that something ominous is watching, and not so far away. I whirl around ... and meet eye-to-eye with Blackie, once again sitting on his ample haunches and just a few feet off the trail I came down only seconds ago. And again it strikes me that he is hunting, in this case looking to ambush bed-bound elk, and I'm flattered that my own predatory tactics, once again, seem to match his. And I'm especially thankful that while he could easily have ripped my face off as I slouched so close and carelessly by, he chose not to.

Might my uneasy friend Blackie have felt less charitable toward me, I'm left to wonder, had I blunted him yesterday?

By all indications, Blackie means me no harm. Yet, he *is* a bear. A big, emaciated and no doubt *hungry* bear at that. So again I ask him to leave.

As he did last night the bear ignores me, like women are won't to do, prompting me to chuckle silently at the possibility "he" may in fact be a she.

But the humor is short-lived – this bear is *close* – and once again I string a blunt-tipped arrow, draw and aim at a haunch.

This time the bruin hesitates before hauling himself to all-fours and grudgingly (seems to me) shuffling away — all of a dozen yards away — before sitting back down to resume his bemused staring.

Again, I opt to back off rather than to blunt.

Blackie just yawns, as if to say goodbye, see ya around campus.

What a kick! Certainly, the spicy scent of danger provides some of the juice powering what I'm feeling now. But there's something more as well, something tantalizingly ineffable ... like a disturbing dream not fully remembered. While a part of me wants more, another part is uneasy and just wants out.

Later, back at the shack, I phone my buddy Tom Beck, Colorado's infamously outspoken bear biologist, and recount my recent adventures. Tom agrees with my supposition that Blackie is, or recently has been, a garbage bear, like so many others this bad summer, having lost his instinctive fear of people through repeated peaceful encounters reinforced by food rewards. Even so, Tom cautions, "Habituated doesn't mean harmless." Quite the opposite in fact. Tom suggests that it's probably a good thing I didn't blunt the bruin, as it might have provoked an attack. Furthermore, he warns, Blackie's nonchalance could change to fierceness fast, should elk meat come between us.

"If you kill late in the evening," Tom advises, "stay alert, work fast, move the bagged meat as far as possible from the gut pile and get the hell out before black dark."

Even so, until such time, Beck confirms my feeling that Blackie is apparently no threat.

Reassured, I propose that next time we meet, instead of trying to scare the bear away, I'll just stand and stare and talk to him quietly; see what comes of a quieter, gentler approach.

"And carry bear spray," says Tom.

"I usually do," I confess.

Alas, the remaining days of elk season come and go, and that wished-for "next time" ever comes.

Weeks later, talking with a game warden friend, I learn why.

Shortly after my two encounters with Blackie, a bear fitting his description and just a couple miles from the mountain where we met, was killed by a bowhunter who found him snoozing beside a hiking trail. As the archer strung an arrow, the bear awoke, yawned, stared bemusedly ... and died.

I won't fault the shooter, who was hunting legally and ethically (that is, in season, with a license in his pocket but without the crutches of bait or hounds). Even so, I sure wish now that I'd blunted that overly trusting bear, so that maybe he'd have run from that hunter instead of merely yawning.

As was likely the case with Blackie, one way or another, sooner more often than later, like the Colorado Department of Parks and Wildlife (CPW) bumper stickers warn, "Garbage kills bears!"

Tragically for the bears, it's popular among a short-thinking uninformed few to blame all "nuisance bear" problems in Colorado on a 1992 state ballot initiative prohibiting the use of baits and hounds for hunting. This outspoken minority — including former bait and hound hunters, former bait and hound outfitters, anti-predator hunters' groups (among the worst of this lot, IMHO, are the misleadingly named Sportsmen for Fish and Wildlife and it's incestuous cousin, Wildlife Forever), sheep ranchers (*of course!*) and even a minority of old-school wildlife professionals — reason that "we need to keep bear numbers under control and make them afraid of people" by hunting and killing all of them we can, any way we can.

No matter how fervently argued, such a short-sighted stance defines willful ignorance. Allow me to explain.

For years, even decades, Colorado black bears were hunted both spring and fall. In spring, fresh from den and weak with hunger, they were chased and treed by hounds, then shot like sitting ducks. Or else the den-starved spring bruins were lured to smelly baits and shot from tree stands. Most bait hunts and virtually all hound chases were conducted by professional outfitters; business was good and profits were high at a time of year when most outfitters otherwise were out of work.

By contrast, in the fall, only "fair chase" bear hunting was allowed, limited to such traditional, skill-based tactics as tracking, sneak-hunting, ambush and spot-and-stalk. No baits. No hounds. In practice, most fall bruins were killed by deer and elk hunters who had a bear license in their pocket, just in case, and happened to get lucky. Others are killed over the gut-piles of hunter-shot elk and deer; a still-legal form of baiting.

Gradually, it came clear to state bear biologist Tom Beck and others, within and without the CPW, that baiting, hounding and spring bear hunting dishonored not only the prey, but the hunters who participated as well ... and thus, by association in the public eye, all hunters and all hunting. And too, there were serious biological concerns, including especially the selective culling, year after year, of large "trophy" males. With bears (as with any wild species), strong arguments exist for leaving a healthy number of prime male breeders out there to pass along their survival-tested genes. But with spring baiting and hounding, every year the biggest bears in Colorado were getting smaller, since the patient hunter sitting over a bait bucket could patiently watch various bears come and go, come and go, day after day, and in the end kill the biggest. Treed bears offer the same "take this little one or wait until a bigger one is treed" selective choice.

Yet, from the public's point of view, an even more pressing and poignant concern about spring bear hunting was the orphaning and certain death of infant cubs. Frequently, a cautious sow will leave her infant cubs in hiding, often up a tree, while she visits a bait station, making it impossible for the average hunter to recognize, before the fact, that he's killing a nursing female. First-year cubs, orphaned in the spring, are absolutely doomed to die, if not from predation, then from starvation. Consequently, "Kill the mother and the cubs die too" became the battle cry for spring hunt critics. Defenders of the status quo, within CPW as well as without, objected that such little deaths did not affect the total bear population of Colorado — in bio-speak, the "resource base." And likely they were right. Yet, to a lot of folks, and a lot of hunters among them, the fate and dignity and manner of death of individual animals matters a *lot*. (In primal cultures, this view that all life is valuable in and of itself, aside from any value it may have for humanity, is called animism; today, it's known as deep ecology.)

Nor is death a good teacher. Many bait-addicted bruins who manage to escape the bullets and arrows of their would-be ambushers (generally by visiting the baits at night) go on to become garbage bears, having been spoon-fed a taste for human foods. Rather than instilling fear of humans in bears, as the pro-baiters claimed, an addiction was being nourished and a menace created. All things considered, something had to give.

For years, CPW professionals and a core group of concerned citizens (none of whom, contrary to pro-baiter claims, were in fact antihunters) had petitioned the Colorado Wildlife Commission (CWC) — a politically appointed, rule-making council of eight — to end the spring bear hunt, citing the reasons listed above and more. But the CWC, blindly loyal to their traditional clients (including outfitters; self-serving and ecologically care-less "We want more" hunters' groups; along with predator-phobic ranchers, of course), responded with denial, arrogance and even childish insults to the petitioners. It got so bad that the well-respected outdoor writer for a leading Colorado newspaper dubbed the CWC in general and their chairman in particular "brain-dead political hacks."

This continued until 1991, when, with their resolve stiffened by years of abuse, an ad hoc group of frustrated Coloradans took form. While a handful of concerned nonhunters were the movers and shakers, they had strong support from ethical hunters and most CPW biologists ... but not one red penny's backing from any animal rights, aka antihunter group. Calling themselves CUB (Coloradans United for Bears), volunteers (my own self eagerly included) easily gathered enough signatures to mandate a state ballot initiative. Having so long been denied even the most reasonable of compromise ("stop spring hunting, and you can keep hounds and baits" they had offered the churlish CWC, to no avail), CUB decided to go for the whole enchilada.

Come November, Amendment 10 (A10) was embraced by a profound two-thirds majority of voters.

Now, beyond two decades later, a few predator phobics, ranchers and other self-serving slow learners still hoping to reduce a keenly complex biosocial phenomenon to mere politics and scapegoating — continue to blame all garbage-bear problems on A10 while proclaiming the evils of "wildlife management by populism." Moreover, according to these apparently blind and deaf true believers, A10 was all the work of the well-funded and nefarious "antis."

So far from the truth, in so many ways!

A10 was *not* the work of the organized antis, who jumped on the bandwagon only late in the game, after all the real work had been done by CUB volunteers, and only when they recognized an easy win they could *claim* for their own (a common tactic also favored by "hunter's rights" groups).

Granted, populism is imperfect, as evidenced by the fools and overt self-servers we regularly vote into public office (or who get themselves appointed, as in the first Bush Jr. "election," by a partisan Supreme Court). Even so, in certain desperate situations, populism can be a godsend. In the instance at hand, massive flaws existed in Colorado's traditional bear management paradigm. All standard channels of redress by process had been tried and retried and finally abandoned; you just can't reason with unreasonable people, especially minor bureaucrats with inflated visions of their own power. No other "less extreme" option remained. And in the end, in retrospect, the "wildlife-ignorant public" who passed A10 has proven itself to be far wiser than the good-old boys and girls of the CWC and their self-serving "client" cohorts.

It's hard to criticize something that works as well as A10 has worked — for bears, for the ethics and image of hunting, for public satisfaction and (surprise!) for bear hunters in particular. According to CPW statistics, since the passage of A10 in 1992, all indicators have trended steadily in the favor of bear hunters and CPW – including bear hunter numbers, percentage success rate among bear hunters, number of bears killed, size of bears killed and income generated for CPW through bear tag sales. The year 2011, the most recent for which statistics are available at this writing, set all-time record highs by every measure of bear hunter success in Colorado, nearly doubling pre-A10 numbers.

I see two apparent if not obvious explanations for this incredible rise in the popularity of Colorado bear hunting following A10. First, with the activity no longer dominated by professionals — bait-haulers and hound handlers — who tended to stake out the best areas and hoard them fiercely for their clients, bear hunting has been rendered more economically democratic, thus more inviting to more hunters. Second, and perhaps more important, with bear hunting now relieved of the moral stench and public stigma of baits, hounds and orphaned cubs, it is coming increasingly to be viewed by ethical hunters as more honorable, more challenging and (thus) more attractive.

And too, bear hunters are likely killing more bears in recent years because there *are* more bears now. And why might this be? Because there are fewer domestic sheep roaming over Colorado's high country to attract bears, which are routinely shot on sight by sheep men, legally and otherwise. (Traditionally, sheep ranchers offer sheep herders a fat bonus, a bounty if you will, for every bear they kill. Do you think these poor young men from Latin America are going to wait for a bear to attack their flocks before they take action to collect this "free money"?) Statistically and pragmatically, it's undeniable that where sheep numbers are high, bear numbers are low. As sheep numbers decline, bear numbers increase. For this reason and so many more – including the destruction of delicate riparian habitat and other wildlife forage, the muddying and shit-fouling of headwater trout streams, attacks on backpackers and others by sheep guard dogs, and the generally proprietary attitudes and politics of so many sheep men, the grazing of privately owned domestic sheep on publicly owned "wild" lands should have become history long ago.

But back to the heart of our topic: Another positive outcome of A10 for fair-chase hunters and hunting's image is that there's no more public concern about spring-orphaned cubs, with its attendant backlash against all forms of hunting. According to Tom Beck, "Any first-year black bear cub that makes it to September, when the autumn bear season opens, is set to survive the winter with or without its mother. Dens have been dug, the cubs are long since weaned, and they've learned what they'll need to know as adults."

As insurance, it remains illegal to knowingly kill a sow with cubs in Colorado.

And finally, since most bears killed by hunters are killed in the backcountry, it's hard to see how hunting can reduce "garbage bear" problems in small towns and subdivisions ... unless CPW someday decides to allow backyard bear hunting.

Those tenacious few who yet today, with more than a decade of post-A10 statistics and experience to examine, still refuse to acknowledge these incontrovertible *facts,* are hunting's equivalent to the Flat Earth Society.

The true creators of nuisance bears are not the "antis," not wildlife management by populism and not hunting restrictions. They are (1) wildlife habitat and natural foods lost to human sprawl, compounded by (2) careless management of garbage, pet and livestock feed, fruit orchards and more among rural residents and (3) cyclical (and thanks to global warming, increasingly common) wild food failures resulting from such "natural" causes as fire, drought and unseasonable frosts. Simply by observing the weather and its effects on local flora, Tom Beck and others who have seriously studied the situation can accurately predict looming garbage-bear summers. Hunting, or not, is a big fat non-issue.

Like their human counterparts, bears are intelligent, adaptable, highly mobile and opportunistic omnivores. If their natural foods fail, the drive to survive forces them to adapt. With rural subdivisions ubiquitous today, a hungry bear's survival search inevitably leads into someone's yard. If garbage or other goodies (pet or horse food, goats and other small livestock, bird feeders, greasy charcoal grills, etc.) are readily available, they'll be gratefully consumed ... and a "problem" bear is born. *Intentionally* feeding bears is not only illegal, it's magnificently stupid —yet it's alarmingly common, particularly among nonresident seasonal visitors.

The proper and most promising response to nuisance bears is not more liberal hunting laws, not harsher nuisance-bear control laws, but public education, cooperation and a sense of charity to our fellow creatures in hard times.

And looking ahead into the big picture and long run, we as a nation need to quit bickering and take bold overt steps, which means personal sacrifices, to curb the human causes of global warming. When we and the bears can no longer trust even the turning of the seasons to be reliable, life is seriously out of balance and at risk.

"Garbage bears" should not be seen as a problem, but as symptom; a warning sign.

Here in southwest Colorado, the bad bear summer that led to my uneasy pal Blackie's death and countless others (but not a single human death) crested (as Beck had predicted it would) in late August. One evening during that time, while driving less than a mile total on a local county road, a friend and I saw three different bears on three different garbage containers. The same was happening throughout the region. But rather than killing or relocating the desperate marauders, as per usual, CPW officials, feeling overwhelmed, experimented with a far more revolutionary tactic — using the local media to make the problem and its solution clear: Eliminate food rewards, and the bears will go away.

Gratifyingly, a majority of local folk listened and acted. Since most rural homes are served by private trash collectors, people began demanding bear-proof dumpsters. Because compliance required investing in new, sturdier and more costly containers, the collectors at first resisted. But as more plastic dumpsters were wrecked beyond salvage, and more bear-besieged customers raised more hell, the garbage guys came slowly around — first by installing new metal lids on the old plastic dumpsters, then, when that failed, bringing in metal dumpsters with plastic lids (huh?), and finally getting it right with all-metal, bear-proof containers with latch-down steel lids. Within days of implementing that final solution, the affected "problem" bears, including starving Blackie, had returned to the woods.

This is not rocket science, but simple metabolic biology. Bears live to eat, eat to live, and have no time to waste hanging around where no food can be found.

Now, with the undeniable onset of global warming and a seemingly endless set of drought summers upon us, perhaps we can use the lessons we've recently learned to proactively prevent, rather than reactively address, another "problem bear" summer ... although, unlike bruins, our species doesn't always learn from experience.

Yet I remain optimistic. While ending tragically for Blackie and other starving bruins, last summer was an encouraging experiment withal, proving that we *can* live peaceably with bears, anywhere we share the land.

We only have to want to.

In warm weather, bears routinely visit water at midday.

CHAPTER 14

Bears, Straight-up

Yes, you *can* successfully hunt bears fair-chase!

With the voters of some states, like right here in Colorado, taking to the polls to outlaw spring bear seasons and baiting, and with a growing number of hunters freely choosing to find a more rewarding way to bring home the bear bacon than sitting over a garbage dump or executing dog-treed and, thus, helplessly trapped bruins, many "Can it be done?" and "How-to?" questions naturally arise.

To answer the first: Absolutely, bears can be successfully hunted using fair chase methods — insofar as anything in fair-chase hunting can (or should) be assured. As a traditional bowhunter and occasional guide who haunts the Colorado Rockies daily for weeks each fall, and as one who has lived among bears, at times way too close, for well over 30 years, I enjoy multiple close encounters with black bears every year, and I'm not even trying. During some recent years, in fact, I've seen more bears on a daily basis than elk, my prey of choice. So while I don't choose to hunt bears I've seen enough of them for long enough and paid enough attention to their ways, to confidently state that for me, even with a longbow, it would be almost too easy. Thus, I'm confident that by following the advice offered here, from me and from others, most any competent hunter stalking good bear habitat can get it done on his or her own, no unethical crutches needed even where they're still allowed.

Confirming my own observations here in the Rocky Mountain West are those of Tom Beck, who recently retired as Colorado's chief bear researcher after spending more than 20 years trapping, photographing, radio-tracking and crawling into occupied dens with black bears. Tom is a recurve shooter who hunts more than anyone I know who doesn't get paid to hunt, and he definitely has the best interests of ethical hunters at heart (as do I, though some will disagree).

To provide fair representation for hunters stalking the eastern woodlands, I also spoke with Dr. Lynn Rogers, who spent 30 years studying bears for the U.S. Forest Service and others. Rogers is one of only two people I know of to have befriended wild black bears to the point he's allowed, by them, to travel and even sleep with the huge, eerily humanlike omnivores.

Since 1992, when baiting, hounding and spring bear hunting were outlawed by a two-to-one vote margin here in Colorado, Tom Beck has worked to identify methods for hunting bruins that are ethical as well as effective. While he acknowledges there is no panacea — no single fair-chase method for taking bears that's equally effective throughout North America, most of the following techniques should work in most areas during fall.

Habits and habitats

Your first requirement in planning a fair-chase bear hunt, underlying all others, is to thoroughly educate yourself about the natural history (aka daily lives and needs and preferences) of bears in order to take full advantage of the predictability of their seasonal habitat use. Fall bear hunts in most states run during September and October. This coincides handily with the annual frenzy among bears to fatten, most often on hard-nut mast and berries, before going to den. Preferred fall bear foods vary not only from region to region, but due to wild crop fluctuations and failures, year to year. So begin by checking with biologists in the area(s) you plan to hunt in order to learn what's normally on the local blue plate special during archery bear season and where these foods are most abundant. Thus informed, concentrate your early scouting not so much on finding bears, as on finding concentrations of the foods they'll come flocking to in autumn, combined with areas you can access. In the West that's almost always public lands. Elsewhere ... well, if all else fails you can always plan a trip out West, where millions of public acres are bristling with big black bears.

Moving along, just before season opening it's a huge bonus if you can arrange to do some glassing and cautious poking around within the larger feeding zones revealed in your earlier telephone and map research (which may be as large as entire watersheds or as small as localized berry patches), looking not only for actual bears but for their tracks, trails, hair, scat, overturned rocks and logs and other fresh spoor indicative of the microhabitat preferences of local bruins. Mark all such hotspots on a topo map and in memory (I don't use a GPS to mark hunting destinations, but there's no laws against it).

And don't overlook water, especially in the West. Under favorable conditions — hot and dry with limited water sources — secluded, shaded pools with nearby escape cover can be magnets to overheated midday bears. Here in southwest Colorado, I've found that bears use small isolated spring pools virtually daily, summer through early fall, for midday cooling dips.

Finally, be aware that where they have ample room to roam, bears never linger long in any one area no matter how rich and diversified the forage, but will munch a few acorns here, stroll over the hill and nip some chokecherries or sedges there, drink or swim yet someplace else and nap in yet another spot, following a circuitous moveable feast that may span several miles and require from a day to a week to circumnavigate. And then they start all over.

This bruin mobility opens two additional doors of hunting possibility. If you can locate routes connecting one chunk of fall bear real estate with another —saddles are attractive travel lanes for all wildlife;

secretive black bears are also fond of brushy drainages and frequently follow deer and elk trails through heavy cover — you've found a high-odds ambush corridor. And just as with deer and elk, if you can identify high-traffic travel lanes it's generally far more productive to sit and let the game come to you.

Curiosity

A second chink in the black bear's defensive armor is the species' keen curiosity. Put something obviously foreign in a bear's universe, so long as it's not overtly alarming, and he'll go out of his way to investigate. Tom Beck's research has shown that bear "bait" doesn't have to be food, but can be anything that registers on any of a bruin's senses and captures his attention.

Sound: Field research by Beck and others, plus widespread hunter experience, confirm that two types of calling can be deadly effective on bears in all seasons. And better yet, you can make both type calls on the same mouth call. First is the familiar "wounded rabbit" predator call, just as if you were calling coyotes. Second is to imitate the frantic squalling of a terrified cub, simply by working out hard on a standard rabbit predator call – calling louder and almost nonstop, putting all the pain and distress you can into the sound. While predator calls are attractive to bears of all ages, the "cub in distress" tactic works best on adult bruins. Bear biologist Tom Beck maintains that the natural curiosity of bears — not hunger or defensive instincts — is the primary draw of both type calls. Yet, he doesn't argue that any predator homing in on a wounded-animal call is likely looking for an easy snack so it's wise to watch your backside.

An adult boar is wired to kill and cannibalize cubs of his own species primarily because he "knows," instinctively, that destroying a sow's young, which may or may not be his own, will help cycle her back into heat sooner, potentially providing him with increased breeding and gene-propagation opportunities. The maternal instincts of sows, meanwhile, prompt them to assist and sometimes even adopt distressed abandoned cubs, though mostly in springtime. (Dr. Rogers once watched a confused spring sow run helter-skelter chasing after the cub-like screams of a circling red-tailed hawk). Later in the season, however, a sow with cubs may kill unfamiliar, unattended cubs, viewing them as competition to her own. To summarize the calling strategy: In fall you're more likely to call in males using a distressed-cub call, while both sexes are attracted to standard wounded-bunny calls.

Since the high springtime susceptibility of sows to distressed-cub calls could easily result in the unintentional orphaning and death of infant cubs, Lynn Rogers advises against this variety of calling in spring.

Tom Beck likewise prefers fall over spring for bear hunting, no matter the technique employed, since "by September or October even cubs of the year stand a good chance of surviving the winter on their own, while springtime orphans are doomed to death by predation or starvation."

No matter the type of call, predator or distressed cub, the key is enthusiastic tenacity. Put plenty of energy behind your squalls, going for a frenetic, high-pitched sound ... then redouble that frantic enthusiasm if you're trying to imitate a bear cub. Do not, however, mix the two during a single calling session. I once heard a cottontail being killed by yipping coyotes, and it's an incredibly loud and (understandably from the bunny's point of view) passionate scream. Wise as they are, bears have brief attention spans and may lose interest and get sidetracked if the calling is too infrequent, too short-lived or too relaxed.

When conditions allow, among the most effective black bear techniques is to combine calling with spot-and-stalk. After spotting a bear at a distance, try to surmise its travel route and maneuver to get ahead of the bruin along its front-trail. Now set up on the downwind side of the trail and start calling.

Vision: A less well known curiosity "bait" than calling, but potentially as effective, is to use a visual attractant — such as a swatch of white or brightly colored cloth (black bears do have at least some color vision, as proven in tests conducted at the University of Tennessee) suspended high enough to be seen from a distance. To keep bears from becoming bored with your "flag," alternate colors, sizes, shapes and locations from one hunt to the next and, most important, pack 'em out after every hunt. Beck has seen visual curiosity attract bears time and again ... and with his help, so have I, to wit:

One recent July, Tom and I set up infrared cameras at two remote springs. With water as the only bait, across two weeks we got exciting day and night photos of bears, elk, mule deer, wild turkeys and even weasels. And in at least one instance with every species except turkey, the animals were staring, close and directly, into the ground-mounted infrared sensing unit. Why? Because, says Beck, who's seen this happen dozens of times and had predicted it to me, the delicate unit is housed for protection (from weather and wildlife) in a length of sky-blue plastic plumbing pipe, which oddity — perhaps owing to blue being an unusual color in the woods (deer and elk also are believed to be able to see bright blue), captures the curiosity of relaxed animals. Especially bears.

Says Tom Beck: "I've often seen bears totally ignore a stinky bait and go directly to check out that piece of blue pipe. Aside from you and me, they're the most curious critters in North America."

As a close-range, traditional bowhunter, you can take ethical advantage of that natural curiosity by employing stimulating sights and sounds, as well as such natural attractants as natural foods, water, game trails and saddles.

Scent: Not only are bears the most curious critters in the woods, they have noses to match. Therefore, positioning your ambush or making your stalk absolutely downwind is mandatory, as is minimizing the spreading of human scent throughout your hunting area. Contrary to widespread misconception, bears do have reasonably good eyesight, probably on a par with our own, and should be granted the same visual respect as other big game species. Wear full-body camo or earth-tone clothing where it's legal and safe. Don't skyline or sunlight yourself. Choose hides with dense, dark backgrounds to avoid silhouetting yourself against backlighting. And minimize your movements, even in a tree stand.

Memory

Aside from compensating for a bear's well-honed defensive instincts, also be aware of their learned behaviors. Bears are creatures of habit with photographic memories when it comes to food and danger. Consequently, if you see a particular bear feeding in a particular location during September this year, chances are more than good (assuming he's still alive) that the same bear will be back again — same place, at more or less same time — next year as well. And so, perhaps, should you.

On the down side of the memory coin, bears never forget places where they've encountered danger, and will avoid or at least carefully inspect all such locales before approaching. I recently saw this phenomenon in action when a hyper-cautious blackie appeared while I was sitting in a long-abandoned permanent tree stand I'd found on public land overlooking a remote spring pool and elk wallow. Approaching on a bold game trail, as it neared the tree in which the stand was located, the lanky dark-brown bear stopped, looked up and stared directly at the stand, and thus at me. I was well camouflaged and hadn't blinked an eye or made a sound, and scent was not an issue as I was downwind in a tree and he hadn't yet cut my ground trail approaching the tree. Clearly, the animal knew the stand was there and that it meant potential danger. After long deliberation, the clever bruin went with his instincts and opted to forego the tempting water in favor of a fast retreat back the way he'd come.

Lesson: Don't use permanent stands for bear — ground or tree, old or new — and vary the location of your set-ups from hunt to hunt.

Regional variations on the theme

Out West, where the terrain is typically a mosaic of sage flats, mountain meadows, dense forests and brushy edge cover, feed plots can be widely scattered, forcing bears to travel a lot, often passing through or grazing in open areas where they can be spotted from a distance. Consequently, western bear hunting frequently imitates western mule deer and elk hunting, with spot-and-stalk being a favored fair-chase technique.

Here too, scouting is critical. Rather than just plopping yourself down on a scenic vista with binoculars and a spotting scope, invest first in some serious back-road driving, backcountry snooping and map work to identify likely feeding zones and the travel corridors connecting them. These are the places to watch. And as previously mentioned, spot-and-call can often be made more lucrative, allowing the bowhunter to terminate the stalk prior to the iffy, last-few-yards stage, by setting up a solid ambush and calling the spotted bear in.

Easterners face a different scenario. Here, bear habitat tends to be more limited in area but richer, restricting bear travel. An exception, Lynn Rogers points out, is northern Michigan. There, bears have more room to roam and they use it. Also, nut-bearing trees and brush there are few and scattered compared to many other eastern states and by September most berries are done for. Even so, even in Michigan, Rogers generally agrees with Beck on the efficacy of fall food-plot hunting, noting that "hazel nut, mountain ash and oak stands become highly attractive to eastern fall bears, as does clover. And in good years such hardy berries as high-bush crans, dogwood and others can last well into September."

Consequently, easterners can successfully hunt bears much as they hunt whitetails, scouting to identify high-use habitats and travel routes, then setting up careful bushwhacks in the best of such places. Eastern-ers may also want to try flagging and calling. But beware: Calling un-seen bruins in the thick cover typical of most eastern hardwood forests, especially in low light conditions, can be excitingly unpredictable.

Timing

East or West, if you have only a limited time to hunt, think about when as well as where to invest it. Fall-fattening bears feed up to 20 hours a day, but the greatest activity — and therefore the greatest hunt-er opportunity — occurs during the last two or three hours of daylight. Therefore, if you can hunt only part-time — say, before or after work — you'll do well to concentrate on evenings, hanging in and hanging out to the last drop of good shooting light.

On a broader timing scale, consider when berries and mast (or oth-er primary fall bruin foods) peak in the area you plan to hunt. That's the time, the week or so, to be there. And when do the leaves fall? Tradi-tional bowhunters, who have to get real close, can use the denser cover and quieter ground conditions before leaf-drop to best advantage.

In sum

No matter the region hunted, the basics are the same: Think when and where as well as how. Take into account your quarry's sensory strengths and weaknesses, natural curiosities, fears, habits and season-ally determined habitats. Do your homework — talking with biolo-gists and other locally reliable contacts, studying topo maps, reading and learning about the daily lives of bears — as well as field (scouting) work. Be persistent, patient and picky ... and you might well get a go at the king of the mountain. Envision this realistic scenario:

After determining a general area for your hunt – a state, country, na-tional or state forest – you phone the state bear biologist who suggests certain foods, areas and times, as well as putting you in touch with the local biologist or wildlife manager for that area. After talking to these local experts, you turn to studying maps and talking with local hunters, thereby narrowing your search down to the few most promising places. As the season nears, you scout those areas and, finding fresh bear spoor, settle on a brushy berry flat as your first choice. A mile to the east stands a scrub-oak acorn grove, also replete with fresh bruin sign. Connecting these two feeding sites is an active game trail crossing a timbered saddle. Due to a lack of suitable trees at either feeding site, you select ground hides at both places, taking into account wind patterns, bear travel routes, shooting lanes, light and cover. In a big pine near the top of the saddle, just downwind of the game trail, you opt to hang a tree stand.

Opening day you work the berries, watching and waiting in patient silence. Next time out you hit the acorn oaks, hanging a curiosity flag from the top of a tall bush exactly where you want your bear to appear. Next time, you try the tree stand in the saddle and maybe throw in some calling. And so on, mixing and matching every trick in your predator's bag while spreading yourself and your scent and disturbance thin from hunt to hunt.

And bottom line, bear or no, you'll have won the game because you'll have truly hunted.

CHAPTER 15

The Yankee, the Antihunter and Me

Author's note: Occasionally, not very often, after archery elk season is done I will guide a rifle-hunting friend from another part of the country on his first elk hunt. I'm motivated to do this in part by the mentoring urge so many older sportsmen come to feel, and in part because even a rifle hunt is a lot more fun than sitting home watching my toenails grow during the prime outdoor weeks of mid-October through mid-November. Similarly, at times I'll join rifle-hunting friends in their camp for an evening or two of good woodsy conversation and camaraderie (and yes, whisky and cigars if it's the night before opening day). The hunt recounted below was unusual in that it combined both of these fine excuses – guiding a new elk hunter and visiting with an old hunting friend – to get out there again.

When I sneaked a glance his way, I saw that the Yankee was staring into the treetops, oblivious to the poster-boy 5x5 bull elk posing broadside in a lemony patch of sunlight a few dozen yards away. On the Yank's behalf I must say that the golden carpet of freshly fallen aspen leaves had allowed the bull to appear in total silence; you'd have to have been looking to see him come. In any event, there was nothing for it but to try whispering across the 20 yards between the Yankee and me — "*Steve!*"

The Yank's only reaction was a bemused yawn. With his attention fully captivated by the comic antics of two iridescent magpies cavorting in the fir boughs above him, he clearly hadn't heard me.

"*Steeeve!*" I hissed, upping the volume to the reckless edge of disaster. "There's a *bull* right *there!*"

Still no response from my Connecticut guest, his face tilted blissfully skyward as if in prayer — a tactic (prayer) I was seriously considering at this point myself.

The bull, of course, got the message this time and went from watching the bird-watcher to glaring at me. But still, the 5x5 held his ground.

By now — cross-eyed with frustration and stone-blind crazy on the rutty stench of the nearby bull — I stood and pumped a thumb franticly elkward, like a hitchhiker on speed, and commanded in far too loud a voice: "*Steve! Please shoot this stinking bull!*"

And still the Yankee — unseeing, unhearing and apparently blind and deaf in the nose as well — remained aloft in his own private bird land.

The wapiti, of course, was more attentive to my dramatics, promptly showing me the north end of a southbound bull.

This was the second morning of our second elk hunt together. I'd guided Steve for a week the year before, but the wapiti had gone to ground the whole time, nowhere to be found. Now, like a thousand-dollar bill skittering down a breezy street, this gift bull had come our way — only to escape our clumsy grasp and blow right on by, indeed, like paper on the wind.

After indulging in a brief tantrum of muted cursing, I sagged over to where Steve was sitting — looking rather forlorn now, since his birds, amidst all the excitement, had finally flown the coop. "Well," I said calmly, attempting to restrain my fuming frustration, "I'm afraid you may never get another chance like *that* one."

"What?" said the Yankee with a start, as if jolted awake from a dream. "Did I *miss* something?"

By now you may be thinking my pal the Yank is hardly the sharpest arrow in the quiver. Think again! His handicaps that morning were inexperience as a big game hunter and an incompetent guide who had positioned himself too far from his shooter. In his limited elk hunting career prior to this day — one week total — Steve had yet to even glimpse one of these semi-mythical creatures that litter the woods each night with fresh poops and tracks, yet can magically go unseen, hour after day after week. Little reason, in the Yank's brief experience, to remain hyper-alert, since "nothing happening nowhere" had, until just now, been the name of the game for him so far.

Besides, Steve had an elk-hunting "expert" at his side. Or he should have. I'd forgotten that my friend was a little hard of hearing. We should have been sitting closer together, within easy whispering and even nudging range — my fault, not his, and our ultimate undoing. We all have to learn, and my continual screw-ups, in hunting as in life, stand as living proof that the learning never ends.

So, while the Yankee loves birds, he's certainly no bird-brain. In fact, "Steve" is Dr. Stephen R. Kellert, a world-renowned Yale sociobiologist and writer who, just weeks before, had delivered the keynote address to a global conference of scholars in Hong Kong. Nor is he a babe in the woods. His most recent summer vacation, for an instance, was spent in the Northwest Territories camping, fishing and floating one of the remotest rivers in North America.

And too, there's the "Kellert Study."

In the mid-1970s, Stephen Kellert gained international recognition by conducting a landmark research project commissioned by the

U.S. Fish and Wildlife Service. In the course of this three-year, multi-pronged investigation, Kellert and his team of graduate students surveyed 3,200 Americans — a random mix of hunters, nonhunters and antis — regarding their feelings and behaviors toward nature. To get at the truth, Kellert employed tests, questionnaires, in-depth interviews and direct field observation. The project produced five reports totaling more than 600 pages, covering an array of topics including people's views on endangered species, predation, zoos, pets, hunting and more.

What has become the most celebrated and significant of those five reports was published in 1978 under the formidable title "Attitudes and Characteristics of Hunters and Antihunters and Related Policy Suggestions." The importance of this 58-page report was in providing for the first time a reliable overview of who we are as hunters, plus who our harshest critics are and why.

Among hunters, and acknowledging considerable overlap, Kellert identified three general types. The largest segment, some 44 percent, fell into what he tagged the "utilitarian/meat" category. Mostly rural males, they were older, less educated and less affluent than the average American. While they did reasonably well on "animal knowledge" tests, the utilitarians shared a cold, product-oriented view of nature — as evidenced, for instance, by their fondness for such objectifying and emotionally distancing agri-industrial terms as "crop," "cultivate," "harvest" and "renewable resource" when speaking of wildlife, hunting and killing. Such euphemisms may make some of us feel better about what we do, but they don't fool our critics and, IMHO, they disrespect our prey. I refuse to use them.

The second hunter type — 39 Percent — Kellert dubbed "dominionistic/sports." These were mostly middle-aged suburban males who knew and cared little about nature, including the animals they pursued. To this group, "the hunted animal was valued largely for the opportunities it provided to engage in a sporting activity involving mastery, competition, shooting skill and expressions of prowess."

Kellert's third and smallest hunter subset — 18 percent — he dubbed "naturalistic/nature" hunters. On average younger and better educated than the utilitarian and sport groupings, these "nature hunters" included the highest percentage of women, had the highest animal-knowledge scores of *any* group — hunters, nonhunters and antis alike — and related to wildlife "with strong affection, respect and, at times, even reverence." Compared to the utilitarians and dominators, the nature hunters were also far more active in wildlife and wildlands conservation issues. Finally, nature hunters hunted more often and more traditionally, employing less technology or other shortcuts and crutches.

Over in the antihunter column, some two-thirds of self-proclaimed antis investigated by Kellert were eastern, urban and female. Ironically, the average animal champion's animal knowledge scores were virtually identical to those of the dominionistic/sport hunters — in a word: dismal. In what for me is a more pleasing irony, antihunters shared with nature hunters the perception that "an equality and kinship, rather than a hierarchical-dominant relationship, exists between humans and animals." (This outlook, in my own life, I've come to call "neo-animism," though I could just as accurately evoke the contemporary term for this "we are equals in the big pictures of life and death" view of nature among some humans: "deep ecology.")

Beyond these commonalities, two distinct antihunting motivations emerged in Dr. Kellert's monumental study. The *humanistic* anti, Steve learned, is driven by a strong emotional identification with animals — particularly pets and such "charismatic megafauna," or big beautiful mammals, as elephants and deer (the infamous Bambi syndrome). But they don't stop there: By perceiving pets as people and wildlife as free-roaming pets, humanistic antis find it easy to view hunting as "murder." This view, as you might imagine, is more prone to radicalism in their desire to end all hunting.

In contrast, *moralistic* antis are driven not nearly so much by their concern for individual animals as by their conviction that hunting is erosive to the moral fiber of those who hunt. Predictably, the moralists are the folks who most strongly object to, and occasionally try to sabotage, programs that introduce youngsters to hunting. (A few such, admittedly, should be ended, such as Safari Club International's giving children praise and awards for killing pen-raised birds and animals ... just as their soul-dead parents and sponsors do for one another.)

And that, of necessity, is the scantiest of overviews of some very deep and revealing research. But if you find human nature as fascinatingly baffling as I do, then even these shallow glimpses into what the Kellert study reveals prompt deep reflection. No wonder the Kellert report is quoted so often by thoughtful hunting writers, even today, several decades later. It was, in fact, a desire to make my own rancid rumblings at least *appear* thoughtful that had prompted me, back in 1999, to contact the good professor for information and advice. Proving himself immediately to be a "regular Joe," Steve Kellert not only shared with me his research and knowledge, but candidly critiqued portions of what would become my Great American Hunting Tome and all-time best non-seller, *Heartsblood: Hunting, Spirituality and Wildness in America.*

Over the months we corresponded and exchanged phone calls, it gradually came out that Steve had hunted birds and small game "a few times" as a boy, but nothing since and never big game. Then, a couple of years prior to his first visit with me, after decades of studying hunters and antihunters, he'd decided to give deer hunting a try. And he loved it. Moreover, he openly hoped someday to have an opportunity to come West for elk. Now, I'm hardly the gregarious type, especially when it comes to sharing my elk camps. But upon hearing this, I promptly invited Kellert to Colorado. He came that same October. And, as I've said, even though the elk played hooky, the hook was set. "Next year," Steve urged as he left to return to New Haven, "let's try this again."

And thus it had come to pass that the Yankee greeted my gentle scolding for not seeing the Godsend bull with an earnest, "What? Did I *miss* something?"

After explaining just what he'd missed and why, I suggested we give this wooded point overlooking a dry gully a few more hours of silent scrutiny. Besides being laced with fresh elk sign, this public-land honey hole was two steep miles up a convoluted mountainside and happily accessible only by internal combustion engines of the heart-and-lung variety. Consequently, we three young fellers had it all to ourselves — just me, the Yankee and Tom "the Antihunter" Beck (off hunting alone this morning, as is his way and normally mine).

Returning to the hunt with fresh resolve, Steve chose a huge, rust-red ponderosa to sit beneath, in deep shadow, with a sweeping view across the gully, up the hill and through the aspen wood beyond. I stayed put in my own pool of shade, now just a few yards away.

Time passed, as time tends to do.

And now it was my turn to be lost in the ozone when, at midmorning, the Yankee shouldered his 7mm Weatherby Mag, braced elbows on knees, leaned into his 3X Leupold and . . . *Ka-Whump!*

What? Did *I* miss something?

Happily, the Antihunter was hunting near enough to hear the shot and deduce our location. Not so happily, according to Murphy's Law, Steve's elk had expired in the narrow bottom of the gully, belly-up and intractable. Even so, by the time Tom arrived — having optimistically hiked down to camp, then back up to us bearing meat bags and three pack frames — Steve and I were all but done converting a quarter-ton elk to what later would scale at 173 pounds of good clean boneless meat.

As we tended to man's oldest profession, Steve told Tom how he'd spotted the lone cow ghosting through the aspens. "And a cow," he professed, "is what I really wanted," feeling he hadn't yet "earned the right" to kill a bull. Coolly if not calmly he'd waited for the inbound animal to enter the gully and drop momentarily out of sight before making his move. But the instant she topped-out on this side, she smelled a rat and put on the brakes. "When she looked at me and started to turn back," he recalled, "I knew it was then or never."

Steve had the cow dead to rights in his scope, and her instincts, good as they were, proved just a moment too slow. And thus was the birdman redeemed.

What Steve *didn't* recall for Tom were the profoundly mixed emotions he'd struggled to express to me when we first laid eyes on his first-ever dead elk — her own eyes still bright and lifelike, mirroring the mid-morning sun, though she was utterly dead. What Steve had said then was that while foremost he felt satisfaction and pride, those joyful emotions were underlain by a dizzying swirl of other feelings, including "sorrow without regret, and *gratitude* ... to this awesome animal, to this gorgeous place that gave her life — the mountains, the forest, the natural cycles of productivity and consumption — and to a larger creation that includes not only elk and elk country, but *me* as well."

Of course, such honest, thoughtful feelings arising in the emotional wake of a kill are scorned by some as "touchy-feely nonsense." Consequently, they're often suppressed even by those of us who regularly experience them. But as one who's killed many elk across many years under many circumstances, and guided many others to do the same, I feel qualified to testify that feelings of the sort confessed by Steve Kellert, whether openly voiced or not, beat at the very heart of the hunt for all the truest and best hunters I've known: "nature hunters," fair to say. Where is the alleged "nonsense" in feeling and acknowledging respect and gratitude to the animals we kill, just as hunter-gatherer cultures the world over did for thousands of years? What's so touchy-feely about consciously recognizing our visceral *connection* to the animals and the places we hunt them in?

Let me tell you: When you kill something big and beautiful and cut it open and stick in your arms in up to your chin and rip out its steaming guts and cut up its flesh and carry it home and eat it and it thus becomes a *part of you* — not only physically but, consciously or not, spiritually as well — well, acknowledging the weightiness of all of this is neither trivial nor somehow "unmanly." Quite the opposite, in fact.

Tom Beck, his crusty tough-guy exterior hardly hiding the huge heart within, didn't need a retelling to know how Steve felt. He could see it in the professor's trembling hands, in the moist gleam of his eyes. And in the big smile on the Yankee's face. But enough of that *woo-woo* sissy stuff, eh?

By deboning the meat and shouldering mulish loads, we resigned to complete the pack-out in a single haul — wapiti, gear, rifles and all. As we tottered down the rocky, ankle-twisting slope, Tom helped distance us from our multiple aches and pending sprains by poking friendly fun at the increasing number of hunters, many of them decades younger than ourselves, who argue that without horses, you "must" have an ATV in order to retrieve an animal as huge as an elk.

An odd bird, my friend Tom Beck. Like Steve, Tom's I.Q. approaches Satan's body temperature. But Tom has deep-South roots and delights in switching that self-professed "Bubba" part of himself, and the accent to go with it, on and off to fit audience, occasion and mood. Relaxed among friends, he's a pure-bred hick. But in front of an auditorium full of people or on the printed page or in a public meeting, his vocabulary is stunning, his diction flawless and his intellect and wisdom undeniable. And neither aspect of the man is fake. As one wry observer once summed him up, "Tom Beck is an intellectual in overalls."

What makes Tom's ATV-bashing so ironically comic is the fact that he suffers frequently debilitating foot and back pain — the latter earned as the wages of a career spent hiking deep into the mountains in late winter then worming head-first into occupied bear dens, wrestling the occupants out, horsing them around for a while in the name of science then stuffing them gently back in. But pain aside, Beck – who hunts with recurve and compound bows as well as a rifle – not only packs out his own game but eagerly assists others as well, viewing "the haul" as a valuable element of the hunting experience. Just two weeks before, he'd helped his hunter-wife Sandy shoulder 220 pounds of boned elk ("*Big cow!*") from near timberline the two miles down to camp, two round-trips each. That caper laid him out for days. But here he was again, playing meat mule and good-naturedly braying to relieve our minds of the weight on our backs.

Unlike my friend Tom, aka "the Anti" (explanation to come), I am no such stoic. Even so, six weeks earlier, I'd enjoyed three vertebrae-crushing go-rounds to pack out my own elk, an equinox cow I killed rifle-fast with a pass-through heavy hickory arrow from 11 yards. Now, laboring under my share of Dr. Kellert's cow I was painfully reminded of how my first September load had been so recklessly heavy — both front quarters (bones still stupidly in), both backstraps, both tenderloins — that after I'd laid down in the aspen leaves to buckle myself into the bulging pack, it took several tries and some inventive contortions just to get up off the ground, and how an arthritic spine, hip and shoulder had me crabbing around like Quasimodo for a week thereafter. But more lasting than passing pain — and here is what Tom knows too — are the lifelong memories of how *good* it feels to do it *all* yourself and do it well, scouting to cutting and wrapping the meat.

Soon enough, with only one brief sit-down break, we were back at camp, weighing our pack loads on Tom's scale and snapping hero pictures.

In unanimous agreement that handling one elk a day is plenty enough, we lounged around camp the rest of the afternoon, dining that evening on Chef Tom's chicken-fried pronghorn with stir-fried veggies

and spuds. For dessert, we drank Tennessee sour mash and jawed about
. . . what?

What in the world might such an odd-lot bunch as we three — an
Ivy League Ph.D., an M.S. in biology who wrestles bears and bio-pol-
itics for a living as a state wildlife biologist, and an unemployable elk
bum who's credentials are limited to B.S. and S.O.B. — what had we in
common to jackjaw about?

Women! Food! Drink! Music!

But mostly, we talked about Hunting.

It was while treading this latter trail of gab that the modestly oiled
Yank asked the well-greased Anti, "What do you plan do when you retire next summer?"

"Hunt a lot more!" came the shrill response, faking outrage, as if to
say "Whaddya *think* I'd do, play *golf?*"

"Geeze, Tom," I interjected, "you *already* hunt more than anyone
I've ever known who doesn't get paid to do it."

Which accidental invitation prompted Tom, not well known
for modesty – to launch into a tally: "Let's see — this year I opened
with bow season but didn't kill an elk because nothing worth an arrow
showed up."

Biologist Beck, I should note, is outspokenly against targeting
prime bulls and bucks during the rut because "We *need* those big boys
out there as breeders." Being one who walks his talk, Tom kills only
cows, calves and the rare young stud "with obviously inferior genes."
This year, "nothing worth an arrow" refers to two 320+ 6x6 bulls broadside at 10 yards. Some folks think he's crazy.

"But," Beck rolled on, "I did get a muley doe with my bow, plus a
rifle doe antelope, a fall turkey and a dozen blue grouse, including three
I popped with a .22 while helping Sandy pack out her cow. That's it so
far. After this hunt I'll have just enough vacation left to duck down to
Arizona with Sandy for Coues deer over Christmas. Then . . . well, you
know, a man has to work sometime. But when I retire . . . "

"Well then," challenged the Yankee (it had been Tom who'd hung that teasing moniker on Steve and now, I sensed, payback was at hand), "if you hunt so much, why does Dave call you 'the Anti'?"

To spare the bashful Beck another bout of boasting, I explained to Steve that in his overlapping roles as a senior Colorado Division of Wildlife (now CPW) biologist, gonzo hunter and self-appointed cultural critic, Tom has frequently voiced personal opinions that seem almost calculated to ruffle the feathers of a fine-feathered and thick-skulled few. Consider such heresies as this, from a speech titled "The Amorality of Wildlife Management," which Tom delivered face-to-face to a national convention of professional wildlife managers in 1995:

"The notion of fair chase is key to the nonhunting public's tolerance of hunting. Most of our critics are not antihunters but just concerned people predisposed to object to what they perceive to be unfair. It's difficult, for instance, to condone the orphaning of bear cubs in the spring. And anyone who's witnessed a pack of hounds tearing apart a bear or lion cub is going to find it difficult to condone hounding. And where is the sport in shooting a bear with its head in a bait-bucket of Twinkies? Most hunting can be ethically defended. Some cannot. Change, where necessary, is our only hope for survival. Antihunters may hold a spotlight on our behavior, but *through* our behavior we control what they see."

Enraged by such blasphemy, Beck- Bashers from within the Bubba hunting ranks fired off angry letters to Tom's bosses accusing him of being a raving anti and demanding that he be fired.

"And thus," I concluded for Steve Kellert, "did our buddy Beck here earn the nickname 'the Antihunter' among his friends with the Colorado Division of Wildlife, all of whom knew the truth."

Later that night, as we wobbled off to our bunk tents, the professor commented eloquently on the "preternatural pinkness of the moon," forecasting that it "presages snow or rain" ... and then surprised us with the announcement that with his hunt finished early, he really had no choice but to return forthwith to Yale and "nagging obligations."

"Now why would you go and do that?" Tom teased, "when you could stay here and enjoy our *fine* company, cook our meals, wash our dishes and help us pack down the elk I'm gonna kill in the morning?"

"It's a tough choice," quipped the wily Yank, ducking for the shelter of his tipi tent.

Come morning, we walked down to our vehicles and I drove Steve to the airport while Tom hauled our friend's elk home to age in a refrigerator reserved for that purpose. (A week later we'd cut, wrap, freeze, pack with dry ice and FedEx a huge insulated box of wapiti flesh to New Haven, C.O.D.)

Back on the mountain that evening, Tom and I enjoyed leisurely separate solo hunts, but to no utilitarian avail.

Tuesday morning — 6 November, Sandy's birthday and Election Day (we'd already voted by mail) — all was changed. Steve's "preternaturally pink moon" had in fact "presaged snow or rain." A little of both, it turned out, lasting half the night. Come morning, Tom loaded up with a day's provisions and in full darkness melted silently into the soggy woods, beneath a clearing sky.

As for me — with a freezer already fat with wapiti, pronghorn and grouse —my motivation to kill another elk, especially with a rifle, was wan. The hunt itself, the friends, the camp, the conversation and laughter, even the gutting and the packing — these were my prey this time out. Unless, of course, I stumbled onto a yummy calf, the elusive "spoon meat" I was at the time obsessed with (after finally eating one, I would get over it) and had sought unsuccessfully through the past four archery

The Antihunter fries up fresh elk steaks for camp dinner.

seasons, having to settle for three stinking bulls and a fat young cow instead.

But happily, no calf was forthcoming, and in obedience to my apathy I returned to camp early from my walkabout and was relaxing tent-side in the warming sun, devouring poetical wild-game gastronome Jim Harrison's deliciously ornery collection *The Raw and the Cooked,* when I was ambushed by a familiar voice crooning "I reckon you'll need your packframe and a couple of meat bags if you want in on the fun."

"Damn," I retorted, feeling guilty for not having returned Tom's favor after Steve's elk went down, "I didn't hear the shot."

Back up on the mountain, well above where Steve had taken his cow, as we prepared our initial meat loads, the Anti gave his tell:

"I was sneaking along a ways below here when I heard a bugle. At first I thought it was some poor Joe who'd watched too many elk-calling videos and didn't know the rut was over. But then came an excited bull squeal that was clearly the real thing. A bull bugling post-rut, of course, means he's found at least one cow still in heat. Since one cow's all I needed, I started toward the bugling, got this far and ran smack into a whole herd — maybe two-dozen animals — contouring east and moving fast. I could see flashes of head and hide through the trees but no clean shot. So I hunkered down and cow-called. The main herd kept on going but a half-dozen animals broke off and started toward me, chirping as they came, then relaxed and began feeding — but still no clear shot. Finally, this *perfect* two-year-old cow grazed into the open at 70 yards and when she raised her head with a mouthful of *Carex*, I took her front-on through the brisket. She died on her way down."

And that was that — for two tasty cows, for the infamous Antihunter, for the suavely debonair Yankee and, alas, for the third co-conspirator of the bunch . . . the one they took to calling ... Elkfart.

CHAPTER 16

Minding the Other Scent

Gone ... but no way forgotten

Every afternoon the year around (well, except for hunting seasons), I take our two dogs and myself on a long walk in the woods. My wife does the same every morning. And almost daily a familiar scene replays: The dogs are running flat-out, you know, for the pure doggy joy of it, then suddenly slam on the brakes and come trotting back to sniff the tip of a sprig of grass or brush along the side of the trail, often with noses touching the scent source. Clearly, some interesting smelling something-or-another has passed this way, probably the night before, and come into brief physical contact with the vegetation. If the dogs sniff a moment then resume their romp I figure it was a deer or elk. If however they are motivated to scent-mark the area it seems logical they are reacting to another canid; around here that means fox or coyote since Colorado was long ago deprived of wolves by the livestock industry. (The same industry, indeed, that overgrazed so radically for so long that it led to erosion so severe that it utterly altered the landscape. The same industry that has trashed so many trout streams and damaged so many watersheds West-wide. The same industry that ... uh-oh, sorry, I tend to get sidetracked.)

The point is that even a few molecules of scent deposited by the slightest contact with even a single blade of grass is enough to arrest the attention of a dog at full run. Even in the dead of winter. Even during drought. Even in the rain. Meanwhile, I can place the same scented sprig directly under my nose, even into a nostril, and never smell a thing. Studies have shown that, depending on the chemical composition of the particular scent in question, it can take up to 200 *million* times more molecules to be apparent to a human's nose than to a dog's.

The difference between our sense of smell and a dog's is in fact so inconceivably radical that it's purely impossible to even faintly imagine, much less to comprehend, what animals' scent worlds look like compared to our own. While a dog's scent-world appears in Technicolor, ours by comparison is deep in the dark.

And now consider that a deer's sense of smell is *far* closer to a dog's than to yours or mine. And a bear can out-smell even a bloodhound.

As hunters after anything but birds (thank the gods that turkeys can't smell!), it's something well worth not just thinking about, but acting decidedly upon as well.

The sage advice to "always hunt into the wind" is essential for the traditional bowhunter when on the move or deciding where to place an ambush. But as the example of my two mutts clearly demonstrates, there's more to scent control than wind direction. In this chapter, then, let's consider the other, less-discussed scent issue: the *residual* scent that lingers for hours, even days, after we've come and gone and which we radiate, to paraphrase Sting, "with every breath we take, every move we make" as we hunt.

While we can never totally eliminate our residual scent wakes, we can certainly minimize the quantity of scent molecules we leave behind to alert prey even in our absence. Consider this analogy: A deer that

Sharp-nosed wildlife can scent-bust hunters long after we're gone.

scents us on the breeze from 20 yards will react far differently than a deer that gets our whiff from 200 yards. While the near deer predictably will flag and flee, the more distant deer, not feeling immediately threatened, is likely to overrule instinct, stand its ground and try to sort out the distant threat visually. And how does a deer know by nose alone whether we're 20 or 200 yards away? It knows by the *strength* of the odor: The stronger the stink, the closer the stinker. Likewise, an animal that encounters a strong *residual* scent on vegetation equates that strength to freshness and that freshness to proximate danger, sparking instinctive flight. Meanwhile, that same deer, upon scenting a *faint* residual whiff of humanity equates the faded aroma with time gone by and, like the distant deer, is a lot more prone to hang around and try to gather more information before expending precious energy in flight.

Knowing this, it's incumbent on us to minimize our scent emission *and* transmission to objects sufficiently to fool keen-nosed prey into thinking we're farther away than we are (odor emission control), or that we passed through some time ago when in fact we're still nearby (odor transmission control). For those who hunt the same piece of landscape or from the same spots, tree or ground, day after week and come and go along the same paths repeatedly, concerted efforts to minimize both emission and transmission of human scent are essential to keeping game in the area, relaxed and following normal patterns (like tending a scrape line). While "active" human scent on the breeze can ruin *a* hunt, persistent residual human scent in an area can ruin an entire hunting season. Therefore, with scent as with sound and sight, our job as close-range stealth hunters is to not let our prey know it's being hunting, or that we were ever "there," even after we've long gone home.

Toward that end, here are some commonsense strategies that maximize woodsmanship and minimize chemical and other high-tech "hunting products" advertised to eliminate human odor (whether they do, or not).

Minimize scent on body, clothing, and gear: While we can't totally avoid chemicals in this modern world short of "going primitive," we can certainly minimize our reliance on chems for hunting. Happily these days, unscented body and laundry soaps are widely available, and not only as hunting products. Wash and shampoo with unscented soap; launder hunting clothes with unscented detergent and, when possible, hang outdoors to dry (unless of course you live downwind of a fertilizer factory); and avoid anything — shaving cream, aftershave, body lotion — having even the faintest "pretty" smell. Of course, such freshman-level precautions are SOP for experienced trad bowhunters, right? Apparently not, considering how many folks, mostly males, I've encountered who hit the woods smelling like French Avon ladies yet apparently thinking they are odorless. Most often, I believe this inability to smell ourselves and our world inflicts those among us whose noses have been crippled by everyday exposure to such common outdoor urban blights as diesel fumes. Indoors, most households brim with heavily perfumed products ranging from laundry detergent to perfume itself (including aftershave). Hunters or not, we would all do well to minimize exposure to strong chemical smells in our everyday lives.

Finally, gear and hardware that can't be machine or hand washed — packs, bows, quivers — should be wiped down from time to time with a clean cloth and baking soda in warm water.

Pay extreme attention to extremities: Feet and especially hands are primary distributors of human smells in the woods. And the contact doesn't have to be direct. Boots in general and laces in particular absorb scent from feet and hands and transfer that stink to vegetation as we go along. Like avoiding walking on oily or other contaminated surfaces with our hunting boots (on the way to hunt is *not* the time to stop for gas), we must keep footwear free of chemical smells; use clean hands (washed, remember, with *unscented* soap) to tie and untie laces; and keep those laces tucked in so that they don't flop around like odor applicators as we walk. To facilitate this end, I dust my feet with baking soda and wear "welded" rubber boots of the L.L. Bean Maine Hunting Shoe persuasion, which leak little if any odor from inside and are easy to keep clean outside. For the leather uppers, I've found Montana Pitch Blend to be a first-rate waterproofing and conditioner, while its natural woodsy ingredients — pine pitch, bee's wax and mink oil — don't seem to alarm game and may even serve as an accidental cover scent. (Every year, in fact, I have elk, deer and/or bears cross or follow game trails I've just used and use repeatedly, without scent spooking.)

Keep your hands to yourself: Minimizing the unnatural odors we bring into the woods, remember, is but half the battle. The other half is avoiding the transfer of those odors to vegetation or other objects we may touch in passing. Of course, we sometimes *have* to use our hands to move brush aside as we fight through a patch of sapling whips, even as we sometimes have to grab a tree to keep from falling when we slip or trip. But we don't have to reach out and gratuitously touch every tree we pass, as if taking tally. And yet we tend to, albeit subconsciously. In addition to wearing clean gloves (I change mine every hunting day) and using forearm or bow rather than hands to push aside obstacles when possible, I've learned to walk with my free hand in a pocket or tucked under a pack strap to keep it out of thoughtless mischief.

Likewise, why push through clumps of high grass, weeds or brush, or let our hats rub overhanging limbs, when such scent-depositing contact can generally be avoided with just a little extra caution and effort? Better yet, if you know you'll be following the same paths to and from a stand day after day throughout the hunting season, go in a couple of weeks before opening day with a pair of garden snips and a handsaw to prune back obstructive vegetation along your route.

Spread yourself around: Beyond cleanliness and avoiding unnecessary contact with vegetation, we can further minimize our residual scent trails by not visiting the same stands and not using the same routes day upon day. By having at least two hide-outs located a good distance apart and rotating between them each time we hunt, we can reduce the frequency of "freshening up" our scent wakes while allowing more time for residual odors to dissipate between visits.

Use *natural* cover scents: *Mea culpa:* When hunting an area I know I'll return to, I use doe and cow pee as cover scents on boots, laces and lower pants legs. And for this, I am ashamed. The problem is that urine-based commercial scents are game-farm products. And game farming is poison to wildlife ethics, fair-chase and the honor of hunting. And when it comes to the urine-collection aspect of this gory business, there are additional serious ethical issues to deal with. (Think about how you'd get a deer or an elk or to pee into a collection container every time they urinate ... and how you'd force them to remain in estrus virtually full-time. If you're familiar with the techniques of veal production, you're on the right track.)

The only way I've found around the foul-smelling moral dilemma of buying commercial cervid pee is to collect it myself, when possible, from female deer or elk killed by me or someone I'm with. Toward that end, for years I carried a pint-sized wide-mouthed water bottle and rubber gloves: After field dressing a donor animal I pricked the bladder and attempted to catch as much urine as possible. Later, I transferred the urine to smaller containers and froze them until time for use. A single full-bladdered cow elk can provide enough natural cover scent to last one hunter for several years (especially if you water it down 50/50, as I do). Why let it go to waste? Alas, it's a sloppy process at best, too often with as much urine spilled as collected. Happily, outdoorsman and writer Dr. Don Thomas has a far better way: "I always carry a 50-cc syringe and a 16mm needle for that purpose," he told me after hearing of my far less professional method. *Eureka!* Why hadn't *I* thought of that? Just poke the needle into the bladder, withdraw the liquid, then squirt it into a bottle for transport. Thanks, Don!

But until we're able to "harvest" that first syringe full of wild-caught game urine, a reasonably effective "low tech" approach to camouflaging human scent is to tromp on every fresh pile of game droppings we come to, stomp around in wallow mud and, for gloves, hats, pants legs and shirt or jacket sleeves, rub down with local aromatic vegetation.

"The more we know," advises Native American wisdom, "the less we need to carry."

Or to buy.

Or compromise our personal ethics and pride and dignity by using.

Don't try to walk and watch at once.
(Branson Reynolds)

CHAPTER 17

The Practice of Silence

For those of us who are into Traditional bowhunting with a capitol **T**, striving to weasel undetected through the woods evolves, with time and dedication, into more than just a necessary bowhunting skill. It becomes – to employ the lingo of Zen – a *practice*. That is, a purposeful and personally meaningful way of interacting with the external world: In this case, to perceive without being perceived. With dedicated application, this quiet, respectful way of entering nature's cathedral comes to feel comfortable, natural, appropriately polite and exceedingly gratifying … we might even say aesthetical (as in artful) and spiritual. That's certainly been the case for me, a hunter whose house of worship is built of aspen, elk, wildness and mystery.

Of course, shifting from spirituality to practicality, nature remains the original and still best natural meat market in the world, and that too — shopping for wild meat — demands a quiet approach … which in its turn demands a different species of "practice" entirely.

Let us speak now to the practice of silence in both meanings of the term: practical and aesthetical/spiritual.

Frankly, too few folks I've hunted with, no matter how woods-wise they might be in other regards, have consistently moved quietly enough to suit me or our intended prey. The blessed exceptions to this complaint, I can count on my bowstring fingers. As I tally it across the years, there are three basic audio-ambulatory hunter categories:

First are those sad-sack souls who are so hopelessly lead-footed that no amount of coaching, cussing or cajoling can muffle their clumsy boots and lurching legs for even a step. These grace-challenged unfortunates, for their own good and everyone else's, would do well never to walk any farther into the deer woods than the nearest tree stand or ground blind.

The second category of walkers I've identified are hunters who've developed the skills and self-restraint required to move in near silence and can do it *when they want to*, but who often get caught up in other aspects of the hunt and relapse into careless crunching. Sometimes this is me.

A third type of walkers are serious hunters who *want* to pass ghostlike through the woods, and therefore are painfully aware of every snapping, cracking transgression they commit – yet, for a variety of possible reasons, have never learned the requisite skills. For all of the above and for what it's worth, here's what works for me, at least when I slow down and concentrate enough let it.

Don't try to walk and watch at once: I put this warning boldly up front because neglecting it can out-shout every other skill in the world of fancy footwork afield. Either keep your head down and study the ground immediately ahead of each step while you're moving, *or* scan your surrounds for orientation or game while standing still. *Never* try to walk and watch at once. It's a guaranteed loser's compromise, later if not sooner.

With that perambulatory preamble and proviso thus prominently proclaimed, let's drop back and start from the ground up.

Modern moccasins: My favorite sneaking boots (I say yet again) are L.L. Bean Maine Hunting Shoes – a venerable, century-old pioneering design that's widely copied these days, for worse but rarely better. "Beaners" have soft, relatively thin but ample gum soles with shallow parallel wavering treads. The welded rubber lowers are utterly waterproof and topped with quality leather uppers and come uninsulated and unlined except for a removable arch supporting foot-bed. Buying half a size large allows you to add or remove sock layers according to the weather and personal pedal preference.

Among the qualities of the Bean Maine Hunting Shoe that most appeal to me are its light weight combined with ample ankle support if snugly laced. Over the years I've hiked hundreds of miles and packed out numerous elk and deer while wearing Beaners, in all sorts of terrain and weather, and suffered nary a twisted ankle or blister (knock on wood). And if you keep the leather uppers well conditioned (I like Montana Pitch Blend, which works well and has a mild natural odor that apparently doesn't spook wildlife) they're as waterproof as anything short of hip waders or milking boots. Another strength of boots with welded rubber bottoms (made not only by Bean but also Schnee and a great many others) is that they're essentially scent-proof if you keep them clean. And best of all for the discussion at hand, the Beaners are stand-outs within their genre for quietness, thanks to sensitive soles that facilitate moccasin-like tactile communication with whatever comes underfoot.

Of course, Maine Hunting Shoes have their weaknesses as well. Being unlined, they're impractical in really cold weather. And the same gum soles that can move you so quietly, are apt to land you on your butt in steep terrain on a wet or snowy day (or night), lacking the traction of lug soles. Still, for early season bowhunting and all things considered, I've found nothing better or even close for sneaking around in nature's garden.

Above the ankles: Dressing for silence doesn't end at our boot-tops. I prefer traditional soft fabrics – wool and cotton – for trousers, shirts, jackets and hats, while my favorite hunting pack, when it comes to quietness, is fleece. (While wool is every bit as quiet as fleece, it's heavier, bulkier and most significantly, far more expensive; out of my financial range.) To the extent it's possible (it's still ubiquitous on "hunting" packs), I've learned to avoid nylon, which loves to yell *Zip!* and *Whack!* as we move through whippy brush. Finally, I always preflight my clothing and gear for rattling zipper pulls, sloshing water bottles, crinkly stiffness and anything that goes *tink* or *clink* in pocket or pack or on bow or quiver.

The approach – phasing in: Like most learning experiences, quiet movement is best mastered by chopping the challenge into bite-sized bits. When I'm super-serious about being quiet in the woods, as I always am when bowhunting big game and turkeys, I find it useful to mentally divide my movements into three categories, or phases, of increasing caution.

Phase 1 is the initial approach. Even though the goal at this point is simply to eat away the distance to your serious hunting grounds, let's say a mile, I begin immediately working to calm my mind and quiet myself. For example, I never slam a door when leaving the truck, but close it as quietly as possible, announcing to myself and anyone with me that it's time to get serious. While I walk fairly fast during the approach stage and I do walk and watch at once, I still take care not to kick a rock or log, step on pinecones or make any other sharp sounds that can carry a good distance. If I have a partner along, we talk little and only in quiet whispers. If I have to cough (which, being prone to allergy attacks, I often do), I stop, turn my back away from where I'm headed, and use a sleeve or glove to muffle the sound as best I can. (I've even been known to drop to my belly and smash by face into the ground to try and muffle coughs and sneezes during a stalk.)

Phase 2 kicks in as soon as I'm far enough away from roads, houses, obnoxious motorized backcountry trails or other sources of human disturbance to begin hearing the subtle sounds and sweet silences of nature undisturbed. At this juncture I mentally and physically down-shift a notch by stopping for a minute to look around, listen and quiet my breathing, truly "hunting" now for the first time. Moving on, the pace is notably slower. I exercise ever-greater care to avoid making noise and I stop more often and linger longer before moving on.

Phase 3 is serious business, whether the final approach to a ground blind or tree stand, the tense conclusion of a spot-and-stalk or setting up on a gobbling tom. It's at this critical point that all the skills we can muster for moving quietly become essential to a successful outcome, beginning with…

Route visualization: Here again, I mentally divide the challenge ahead into three categories. But unlike the three approach phases, which fall lineally one after another, the three elements of route visualization overlap, like so:

The long run: As big game hunters we generally have at least some idea of where we want to go – up to a ridge top, down into a valley, to a secluded wallow or scrape line. To get there as quietly as possible, I start by scanning the terrain and vegetation as far ahead as I can see in the direction of travel, noting likely friendly-walking bits such as green grassy patches, along with such predictably problematic stretches as rocky slopes and snarls of brush. Now I pick out an intermediate landmark in the middle distance and mentally map the quietest-appearing route to that landmark, even if it takes me out of my way or requires extra climbing. If I'm lucky enough to find a game trail heading more or less in my direction, I step lightly onto it and say "Thank you!" Well used game trails are packed firm and generally kicked free of vegetation and forest debris, offering silent, sure-footed avenues through otherwise noisy nightmares.

Detours: As we move along, we'll predictable encounter unbearably noisy terrain, dense vegetation or other obstacles we can't foresee at the beginning, forcing us to detour from the original loosely planned route. When it comes to such impromptu choices, it's generally wiser to walk longer rather than louder. Why, for instance, snap and pop over a limby downed tree, when we can walk in comparative silence around it?

In the short run, closing in, step by silent step: Don't try to walk and watch at once. When we're in the serious soup, in and amongst alert game, it's imperative to identify and avoid every last little likely noise-maker as we inch along – pine cones, stones, dry twigs and such. Let's take a few slow careful steps, and stop. Search thoroughly for game: looking and listening. If the coast is clear, then mentally flag the next leg of the approach, scanning the stretch ahead for the quietest path … then lower our gaze back to the ground ahead of our boots and take a few more slow, silent steps. Move, stop, look and listen, move again: Such is the practice of silence.

Don't just stop – *stop!* A personal tic that still drop-kicks me from time to time is the tendency to shift my gaze and attention from my feet to the surrounding woods a moment too soon as I come to a stop. Often as not when we stop, we pause for an initial moment, then shift one or both feet a little for better balance or to improve the view as we look around … and, having already switched our attention from feet to surroundings, we snap a twig or kick a rock in the process. Train yourself to keep your focus grounded until you are *completely* stopped and situated comfortably.

Go slow: This is so basic it shouldn't need to be said. Yet it does. Once we're out there where the wild things are – approach phases 2 and 3 – anything is possible at any moment, in any location. Consequently, any sense of hurry or destination is counterproductive. Not only does a slower pace make for quieter movement, it allows us to actually *hunt* as we move, rather than merely walking while glancing around and inevitably seeing the south end of a north-bound whitetail. Who among veteran bowhunters has *not* spooked a ghostly deer en route to the stand, or busted an elk or turkey simply by moving a little too fast and inattentively, thinking about where we're *going* rather than where we *are*. Be *here, now*.

Stop often and strategically: Here's another mossy old chunk of basic sneak-hunting truism, yet far too often ignored even by the most experienced. Beyond the obvious benefits of spending more time watching than walking, frequent stops keep the heart rate down, our antennae up and our mood properly predatorily attuned. And why stop like a billboard exposed in bright sun? Pick stopping places strategically, preferably in the shade, where you can see but not easily be seen. Think *visual* silence.

Hunt alone: Try as I may, I've never been able to overcome the tendency to move too fast, thus too incautiously, when hunting with another, including when I'm guiding. And I see the same distortion in others. Perhaps this problem is motivated by a subconscious fear of boring our companions by "holding them back," or an even subtler sense of competition and "getting there first." Whatever, for me it's a predictable truth that hunting with a companion is sloppy hunting compared to what I can do alone. Rather than putting my full focus on moving quietly, stopping often and searching for game and sign, I catch myself moving faster, more focused on keeping track of my companion than on the actual hunt, checking his or her (especially her) body language for clues to things he or she may see that I cannot, or gesturing or whispering back and forth unnecessarily. Thus and so, often as possible, I prefer to hunt alone. You don't see mountain lions, the most silent and stealthy of all big North American predators, hunting in packs. In fact you rarely see lions at all, though they are always watching us. And that is our goal as traditional bowhunters who need to get close: to be good lions.

Take advantage of natural cover sounds: Years ago, before learning that I generally prefer *hunting* big spring gobblers to *eating* them, I had a habit of breaking out the shotgun for the last week of turkey season, if necessary, following several weeks of close calls, missed shots and other mishaps with the longbow – in a last-ditch attempt to "succeed" and make meat. Just so, toward the end of one long, warm, late May day of doing just that, a big wind blew up from the west, huffing in tumultuous gusts punctuated by short silences. Moving forward only when the wind was blasting and rattling leaves, and standing still when it paused, I was working my way slowly through a shoulder-high thicket of scrubby Gambel's oak brush when a tom's head bobbed up close in front; I had almost stepped on him. Because the thick brush allowed the big bird no runway for takeoff, he had to helicopter clumsily straight up, allowing me to make a successful head shot on a flying turkey. In fact, I believe I could have done it (as a body shot) with a bow, had I had an arrow nocked, which of course I would not have while working through dense brush.

In any event, the point is that had I not used the covering ruckus and visual confusion of a strong wind rattling the leaves to mask the sounds and motions of my slow careful progress through noisy brush, I would never have gotten even within shotgun range of a sharp-eared spooky tom. In this regard, a wind in the face is the silent stalker's friend in more ways than just blowing your scent away. Other common cover sounds we can and should use to good results include scolding squirrels, croaking ravens or cawing crows, bugling elk and, alas, even those annoying and ubiquitous airplanes.

Foot placement: On fairly level terrain, all things considered, I find that generally the quietest approach is to place your heel down first, then slowly lower the toe. If you're wearing proper bootage, with soles thin and soft enough to translate subtle messages from ground to foot, and if you're moving slowly enough and maintaining good mental and physical balance, you'll find that you can often feel even a small stick or cone underfoot before you put full weight down and catch yourself in time to shortstop the step and prevent a crunch or snap.

Climbing steep uphill generally dictates putting your full weight on tiptoes with every step, while downhill is just the opposite; these are structural demands of muscles, tendons and balance, hard to avoid and not usually a problem. For descending steep hills with unsure footing – scree, mud, wet leaves or snow – it's best to crab down sideways. This not only puts more boot-edge on the ground with every step, increasing traction, but also greatly improves balance and lessens the chance of noisy slips and falls or dislodging rolling rocks.

Exaggerate boot lift over obstacles: Another area that still causes me occasional self-embarrassment is failing to lift my trailing foot quite high enough when stepping over downed logs or other low obstacles, with the result that the toe of the back boot makes solid contact. *Thud!*

And what else? Hard to say, as the "best" silent walking techniques depend so heavily on individual build and grace, the terrain and vegetation under foot, weather and other variables.

Oh, yes, there *is* one more significant piece of advice worth offering here, to wit: Please and pretty please … don't try to walk and watch at once.

Elkheart's favorite broadhead

CHAPTER 18

Broadhead Basics

The literal point of all bowhunting – the make-or-break culmination of all our target practice, gear preparation, skills acquisition and effort afield – is the broadhead. The right head, scalpel-sharp, can often rescue an otherwise tragic wounding situation (as when, for example, a shot impacts heavy, penetration-limiting bone). By the same token, a poorly designed or dull head can all but guarantee heartbreaking failure, personal embarrassment, bad PR for bowhunting and worst of all, unnecessary suffering among the beautiful wild creatures we so love and love to hunt.

Anyone who fails to honestly put the animals first – that is, take very possible precaution to assure fast, humane kills – has no damn business hunting.

There's no such thing as overkill in bowhunting.

Throughout most of the 20th century, broadhead design was mostly mediocre and steady-on. Back then, even smallish innovations – like bleeder blades or stainless steel – prompted big stirs of excitement within the backwards-gazing world of traditional arrow-slingers. No more. Today, bowhunters, including traditionalists and training-wheelers alike, face a blinding array of broadhead designs and materials to choose from, most of which are wildly exaggerated as "The best broadhead ever!" via advertising hype, embarrassingly unqualified hired-gun "pro staffer" hacks and outdoor magazines sucking hard at the industrial profit teat. While the best of today's broadheads have never been better (that is, more reliably lethal), the worst have never been worse (mechanicals and just about everything you see on the shelves at WallyMort and shamelessly hawked in commercial bowhunting magazines (*Traditional Bowhunter* being the only exception I'm aware of). And so it is, so sadly, that for beginning bowhunters and way too many who feel themselves to be veterans, *informed and wise* broadhead selection has become a boot-camp obstacle course.

In hopes of helping those who place the welfare of their prey over the welfare of their own egos or the comfy but less than optimal rote of "How I've always done it," what follows is a brief history and update of the basic broadhead options and their strong and weak points, offered with as much objectivity as old Elkheart can muster.

Broadhead Designs and Materials

It's generally true that broadheads kill by cutting and bleeding. Yet the goal of every ethical bowhunter should be an arrow set-up and shot placement that combine to achieve *full pass-throughs* that deflate both lungs and as a bonus perhaps cleave open the heart, thus starving the brain of oxygen and killing so fast that blood trails are reduced to colorful afterthoughts because they are not needed. The key question thus becomes not "Which broadheads cut the biggest holes and thus [ostensibly] leave the boldest blood trails?" but rather "Which broadheads produce the most consistent pass-throughs and thus assure the fastest, most painless and ethical kills? With that ultimate goal firmly in mind, and with a skeptical attitude (at best) toward advertising, let's open our eyes and minds and shop around.

Rigid broadheads: Since they have no movable or removable parts, rigid (aka fixed-blade) broadheads are the strongest and thus most reliably lethal of all broadhead designs, past and present. Always have been and always will be. Part of the reason for this, and no small part, is that all rigid broadheads have cut-on-contact points; a *huge* bonus if not an outright necessity for slower-shooting traditional bows. The rigid broadhead's only "disadvantage" is that you can't replace dulled blades but have to resharpen them yourself (or hire it done). But hey, is this truly a disadvantage? For serious hunters and humans, the more we can do for ourselves rather than hire done by others, the more challenges we can overcome, the more skills we can master, the more of ourselves we invest in the hunt or in life, the greater pleasure we take from an experience when it works out and the less guilt we feel when it doesn't. With the great tools and instructions available online today (see the same KME Sharpeners website), anyone who is truly serious about "taking control of our own lives" (to quote an old *Mother Earth News* slogan) can learn to get broadheads scalpel-sharp or better.

Variations on the fixed-blade concept are many. Nonetheless, the basic design — springing directly from the proven technology used to make arrow, atlatl, knife and spear points throughout the long and largely lost legacy of human hunting history — is a flat, symmetrical, two-edged blade with a point designed not to punch, but to *stab* through tough hide and muscle. So perfect is this premiere design that the only significant change in the rigid two-blade broadhead in human history was to replace stone with steel. Talk about "traditional"!

Consider the physics: When was the last time you saw a three- or four-bladed dagger? The dagger blade — long, narrow and flat, with two sharp cutting edges behind a cut-on-contact point — is the most lethal stabbing design the laws of physics allow. Streamlined two-blade broadheads emulate the dagger's sublimely lethal design. Long, narrow two-blades fly well, pierce tough hide with a minimum of frictional resistance, and stab (aka slice) enthusiastically through soft tissues. Likewise, the two-blade rigid design *should be* the most efficient for splitting through heavy bone. I say "should be" because not all two-blades are created equal, and the outcome when metal whacks bone depends on a litany of variables including bone mass, angle of impact, blade width and thickness, ferrule aerodynamics, total arrow weight, angle of edge bevel, point design, and most significantly, sharpness and hardness. And sharpness, keep in mind, doesn't count for beans if the steel is too soft. Among the saddest excuses I hear from hunters in defense of their favorite soft-steel broadhead brand is "But it's so easy to sharpen!" I'll leave it to you to carry that thought to its logical conclusion "when the bullet hits the bone" as the old song says.

Rigid broadheads also come in multi-blade configurations as well as flat two-blade designs, with the venerable three-blade being most popular among the multis — in no small part due to its ease of sharpening. To establish and maintain a consistent edge-bevel angle on a *two-blade* head requires either a sharpening jig, or the exceptionally expert eye and steady hand that come only with informed training and tireless practice. But to sharpen a *three-blade* at precisely the same edge-bevel angle on each edge every time, one need only stroke the head across a file, whetstone or steel, handily sharpening the two inner edges of the two "down" blades at once. By rotating the head after every few strokes, both edges of all three blades are readily beveled to identical angles and a triangular cut-on-contact point is produced. Alas, the slicing angle that results from flat-sharpening is 30 degrees per edge, producing a relatively blunt 60-degree cutting angle per blade. In sharp contrast, the (currently considered) optimal bevel for two-blade broadheads is 25 degrees, providing a notably thinner and therefore sharper 50-degree cutting angle. A three-blade sharpened flat compares even less well against a *single-bevel* two-blade, which, as the name implies, is beveled on only one edge of each blade, therefore halving the total cutting angle in order to do its slicing with an obsidian-thin 25-degree edge bevel.

Four-blade broadheads square off the rigid category. While this design has its fans, it remains less popular than three- and two-blade broadheads. One problem is getting a sharp edge on both sides of four fixed blades — given their 90 degrees of separation — using conventional sharpening tools and jigs. Responding to this problem we saw the mid-century introduction of "bleeder blade" hybrids. Best known of this lot is the Bear Razorhead — a flat two-blade head with a slot through the ferrule to hold a razor-thin insert perpendicular to the main blades. And I do mean razor-thin, as in altered razor blades. Though smaller than the primary blades, these so-called bleeder blades jut at 90 degrees from the larger main blades to create a hybrid four-blade. By removing the replaceable inserts (easily done with pliers), the main blades can be resharpened unencumbered by the add-on wings. Now insert a fresh replaceable bleeder (a single sliver of steel that projects on both sides of the ferrule slot) and you have a nice sharp four-blade. Yet, removable bleeder blades are flimsy and the antithesis of "fixed," and consequently suffer frequent failure, including breakage and separating from the head inside an animal, there to lurk in ambush for probing fingers.

In review, the primary advantages of rigid or fixed-blade broadheads, no matter how many blades, include unequalled strength and cut/slice/stab-on-contact tips. The primary "disadvantage" is that you must either sharpen them yourself or pay a pro to do it. Also, after repeat sharpening sessions, rigid heads (particularly the softer-steel versions, which sadly still dominate the market if for no better reason than nostalgia, habit and ignorance among consumers) lose edge metal, thus width, weight and, potentially, flight balance and penetration potential.

Component Broadheads: The primary sales point of component, or replaceable-blade broadheads, is that they eliminate the need for us to acquire cutting-edge sharpening skills. When you dull or damage component blades, they can be readily replaced with fresh, factory-sharpened blades, most of which in fact are adequately if not stunningly sharp. Naturally, broadhead manufacturers love component broadheads since they create an ongoing aftermarket demand for replacement blades. Alas, a primary weakness of the component broadhead is its lack of an efficient cut-on-contact tip. Rather, we are asked to settle for cones, triangles, wedges or tiny, laughably flimsy "cut on contact" mini-blades mounted out front of the otherwise typically aerodynamically inefficient Big Fat Ferrule. The ferrules of component broadheads *have* to be bigger to accommodate blade inserts and their locking mechanisms. And finally, any time you have anything assembled from component parts, the odds of malfunction and impact failure skyrocket. (I know this personally because I used to fly helicopters, aka "buckets of bolts.")

Mechanical component "open on contact" broadheads: These little disasters fall dead last in our ranking of broadhead reliability and lethality because they have proven — in controlled tests as well as afield — to be the least structurally reliable and (even when they hold together and function as advertised, which is iffy at best) the least lethal of all broadhead designs when driven by medium- or low-draw-weight bows. To put it bluntly, mechanicals have no place in the traditional bowhunting world of relatively slow-moving, heavy arrows. Remember, a mechanical broadhead tip must have sufficient strength and bulk to serve on impact as a plunger or trigger to free the (generally spring-loaded) folding blades. Consequently, an absolutely functionally reliable cut-on-contact mechanical-broadhead tip does not exist (so far as I know). And the picture only gets uglier from here.

Please excuse my overt lack of impartiality on this point, but while the choice to shoot a compound arrow-launching machine can be seen as mere personal preference (and even more often, ignorance of the traditional option) with no moral implications, mechanical broadheads, with *no* exceptions in my studied opinion, no matter type or hype, have proven overall to be the most unreliable, inefficient and consequently unethical gadgets among all "modern" bowhunting contraptions and contrivances. Compounding the problem, these switchblade heads, heavily hyped to "shoot just like target points," when used as they almost always are to front straw-weight carbon shafts, serve to feed the hi-tech craving for speed and lower trajectory in order to attempt everlonger, ever-riskier and obscenely unethical shots. Ineffectively light arrows, poorly designed broadheads, unconscionably long shots ... these rank high among the reasons I constantly speak out again the popular misconception that "modern," hi-tech bowhunting is in fact bowhunting at all.

To date, Oregon, Idaho and Washington have outlawed mechanical heads for all big game. Connecticut requires heavier bow weights for mechanical heads. Alaska does not allow mechanical heads for any of its bigger game species. And many informed bowhunting outfitters forbid them in their camps. Yet these ethical and functional abominations remain legal in most states.

In hunting as in life, if we can't or don't wish to be bothered to do a thing right – especially when that thing bears directly on the lives and deaths and potential suffering of fellow living creatures, and our personal dignity to boot – why do it at all?

But back on topic ...

Steel: We have carbon and we have stainless. While each has its fans, neither has a clear mechanical advantage. Far more important are blade thickness, bevel angle and sharpness, overall shape and strength (that is, mechanical advantage, or MA), and hardness. Current consensus holds that 52-53 Rockwell C is optimal. Much below that range is too soft, thus too easily dulled, bent or broken at the critical moment of contact with heavy bone. Remember please that if "I like this brand of broadhead because it sharpens easily," it also dulls easily. Likewise, much above 53 Rockwell C is too hard to sharpen without special skills and tools, and, depending on blade thickness and bevel angle, potentially brittle.

Coda: That's as complete and objective an overview of broadhead basics as I can muster. As an addendum, knowing that some readers will be curious about my personal preferences: I'm a card-carrying disciple of Dr. Ed Ashby's unassailable, decades-ongoing "Arrow Lethality Study." In *every* instance where I've been able to test his conclusions, they are spot on. (Meanwhile, according to their own testimony, a majority of Ashby's harshest critics have never seriously tried what they so cockily criticize.) Consequently, today I shoot rigid, two-blade single-bevels at or near 52C (never B, which is a lower rating) Rockwell for all big game and even turkeys. More precisely and importantly, I've gotten the best (most consistent, trail after trail, year after year) penetration and lethality on elk with long, narrow, two-blade broadheads, the closer to a 3:1 length/width ratio the better. Finally, again in perfect compliance with Ashby's research, I consistently get the best results with way-heavy heads mounted on light shafts (carbon and Sitka spruce) that conspire to net a total arrow weight of at least 650 grains and extreme forward-of-center balance (EFOC; 20% or better). With this set-up, this year's elk, like many others before (but only since I turned to the Ashby solution) went down within 15 yards and was dead in fewer than that many seconds, while my latest Coues whitetail found his spine totally severed and dropped on the spot.

There's no such thing as overkill in bowhunting.

But for the short answer to "What broadhead do you prefer for elk with your low-50s poundage longbows?" the answer is: The Tuffhead. While there are several excellent, Ashby-inspired two-blade single-bevel broadheads currently available, for me the Tuffhead has the mo-stest bestest stuff in a single package. And best of all, they come so re-markably sharp that you can take 'em right out of the box and put 'em on an arrow and go right out hunting with absolute confidence in their surgical sharpness.

Alas, when it comes to broadhead lethality I have little to no brand loyalty. I want the most reliably lethal, brand name be damned. If an even better unit than the Tuffhead comes on the market tomorrow and I can afford to buy it, I'll switch.

If you'd like to add greater depth to this shallow overview by look-ing into the most expansive and reliable broadhead lethality research available, which I urge you to do, check out the Ashby Library at www. tradbow.com (you'll have to register but it's free). Specifically, see "Ar-row Lethality" (part of the original Natal Study), parts, 2, 3, and 4; plus Ashby's research updates for 2005, part 3; 2007, parts 5, 6, and 7; and 2008, part 7.

Bottom line – and I don't mind being redundant on this critical point – is that we owe the surest, fastest and most painless deaths we can deliver to the beautiful free spirits we hunt. Anything less is a failure of the sacred compact between human hunter and prey.

Last load out (Alex Bugnon)

CHAPTER 19

The Gift

Sometimes, silence *is* golden

Every September for years now when I'm hot into my annual rut, I've dashed off informal and often excited daily "hunt reports" via e-mail to the few friends who have hiked with me through my hunting areas and know the landmarks by the names I've attached to them. Then I forget about the reports and the e-mail "sent" folder eventually gets deleted (I share one computer with my wife and like all things spousal, confusion ensues). Consequently, should I later decide to write or spill out a yarn around a campfire about a particular hunting experience, I'm forced to try and sort out the details from a smear of overlapping memories spanning as much as a month and going back as far as decades previous. And these days the old boy's memory, well, she ain't so photogenic (*sic*) as she once was.

Consequently if belatedly, this past elk season I experienced a light-bulb moment and decided for once to keep copies of my daily e-mail hunt reports – hurried, informal and unpolished as they tend to be – for future reference. Just in case. And from there I decided, what the heck, why not share some of those fresh memories with you. So here we go ...

To Doc Dave Sigurslid (early September)**:** Last night while sitting in my brush blind at Hillside Spring, which (the spring pool) hadn't been touched in 10 days or so, a bull started bugling from down at the bottom of the Meadows and I cow-called to him and next time he bugled he was closer. I called again and this time he whistled from right up the hill behind me, with some cows chirping in the background. I gave another cow call and the bull left his girls and came down to the bench toward the spring. But rather than taking the game trail that runs by my stand, he came crashing down through dense aspen saplings and stopped some 50 yards away, by the old wallow near the bottom of the spring seep, where I couldn't see him for the thick vegetation.

The bull spent close to the next hour there, sometimes crunching around, sometimes silent, and bugled four more times. As you well know, a full-throat bugle from a mature bull at that range is enough to shake the trees! At some point he snuck out and when he bugled again he was well below me, to the southeast, on or near the game trail I take coming and going from my truck. So I got my gear together pronto and was able to hunt him almost all the way out, when he broke off east and crossed Big Gulch and was moving fast and it was getting too dark to stay on him.

After that experience — lots of hearing but no seeing — I really want a look at this guy, to see if he's the 350-category beauty I saw back on September 1st, or a smaller 6x6 I got pictures of last summer, or someone new to the local mix.

Weather of late has been perfect for hunting, with mostly overcast skies, highs in the low 70s and nights in the low 40s. There's a chance of rain every day but so far the few little showers have been so ephemeral that I haven't even had to put my rain suit on. This is prime-time and I should be hunting mornings as well as evenings but rarely do, having so damn much "home work" to keep after, like getting in several cords of firewood for the winter.

That will change on Wednesday, when Alex [Bugnon] arrives from New York for his almost-annual week of chasing elk here. Having someone else to hunt with is really motivating and energizing, though as Alex has learned the local landscape better every year and has gotten the hang of the game, like you and me, he and I hunt mostly apart. He likes to walk as much as I like to sit. And having been raised in Switzerland he views every mountain as a challenge to take on. Walking is interesting and you see more elk, but mostly from a distance and/or running away. And after enough strolling around you've alerted every elk on the mountain to your stinking presence. Sitting is boring unless you have a Zen mind that appreciates every little thing around you at every moment, which I do and so do you. And so does Alex for that matter. And one of these evenings a bull will come in to drink and give me a Christmas shot opportunity. Just like so many times before. Hunting is an exercise in faith ... no, not faith, but optimistic patience.

Anyhow, all of that with the nearby but invisible bugler played out last night. Tonight was even better. Much better, even though I've rarely spent so much time so close to so many elk talking constantly, while not seeing any of them because the vegetation, primarily aspen saplings, is so damn thick. When I parked my truck for the evening hunt, about 4 p.m., a bull was already bugling from up the mountain, somewhere around Elk Spring, you remember that one I'm sure, on the east side of Spring Bowl from Hillside. He ran around in the Bowl between the two springs, bugling all evening and really had the cows going on several exciting occasions, leaving me pinned down for fear of getting busted and causing a stampede if I tried a stalk with all those moving noses out there, like so many pin-balls and shifting breezes to boot. I just had to hope the herd would drift my way. Which of course it didn't. When I finally left at dark, the bull was right back where he'd started, at Elk Spring. Darn it, I'm going out in the morning. Enough fooling around and warm-up time. Time to get serious!

As a side note to my personal physician: I haven't had the crippling leg and foot cramps again, been several days now, but my hands still lock up when writing, tying boot laces, etc. I wonder if I can get through field dressing an entire elk without my knife hand becoming useless? I hope to find out soon. – *Selah*

To Alex Bugnon (a week later): Forty-one degrees this morning, light sprinkles, another perfect hunting morning. But I'm giving the elk a day off.

Last evening was yet another fun time chasing a bugler at close quarters, but frustrating also. I've been going out anywhere from 2:30 to 4 p.m. and straight to Hillside Spring. Yesterday I was a bit late due to having to help Caroline process our annual bushel of roasted green chilis (which, along with elk meat when I'm lucky, always comprise most of our freezer contents going into winter). As soon as I got up the hill from where I park the truck, I heard a bugle that sounded like it came right from Hillside. Then the wind came up, whipping hard this way and that, and it started raining lightly. The closest conifer trees for shelter were over by Elk Spring, so I went there, where I hadn't been for a couple of days, and saw that once again the spring pool had been hit by elk, including a wallowing bull. Sitting out the sprinkles under a dripping fir, waiting for the rain to slack or quit, took about half an hour, during which no more bugling.

Anyhow, when I finally snuck on over to Hillside — approaching on the game trail that comes out just below the wallow, maybe 60 yards below the spring — the bull was nowhere to be seen or heard and it started sprinkling again so I hunkered down under another tree there, where several years ago I'd built a half-assed brush blind overlooking the wallow. The wind continued to shift around and I was nervous about being in there at all, knowing a bull had just been in the area and almost certainly was still nearby. I was on high alert the whole time I was there, close to an hour, but nothing came of it until finally, about the time the wind shifted downhill for the evening, the bull bugled again, from just above the spring — not "above" as per up the ridge along the east edge of the Meadows, but in the aspen sapling jungle up north of the spring, and close. I waited until he bugled again before I started moving, at which point he was headed over toward Elk Spring, where I'd so recently been. These guys are really giving me the run-around this year!

But before I took off after the traveling bugler I went to check the adjacent wallow, which hadn't been used so far this year. And sure enough, it was freshly torn up and stinking! This yet-unseen bull is the most tenaciously local and vocal of several singers I hear most days, so I'd love it if he turns out to be the huge 6x6 I saw back on the first of the month, a rare occurrence indeed. But I'm betting it's the smaller 6x6 that hung around here all summer. What this means is if I hadn't been late in getting up the mountain this afternoon, thanks to the chilis, and had I been in my Hillside hide an hour or so earlier, as usual, I might well be packing meat now.

Oh well ... except for dripping trees the rain had stopped again and the bugling picked up as the unseen bull headed toward Elk Spring. Thanks to the wet ground I was able to move quietly and fast enough to keep up with him in parallel, with him maybe a hundred yards below me to the south. Then suddenly, just as I was narrowing the gap, a second singer chimed in from the east, from over beyond Big Gulch, and the two of them promptly closed on one another and really got into a screaming contest that sounded like a "parallel bugling march" uphill, headed north. I had been doing a good job of moving in on the first bull through the thick stuff and had gotten close enough to nock an arrow, but now the pair headed uphill too fast to follow, and the day's light was going just as fast the other way. So I said shucks, backed off and started down toward the truck—when a *third* bull let out a particularly deep-throated scream from down in the dense little valley below Hillside on the north and the Meadows to the west. He seemed to be cheer-leading the other two without participating. My cow calling had no apparent effect on him, just as it hadn't on the two vocal combatants.

And so it was that I felt a little agitated when I got home and heard myself grumping to Caroline, "I've had enough *fun* already. It's time for some *action*." Having sat in ambush, not always comfy, for some two weeks, to have an elk finally show up right there in the bulls-eye zone and for me to miss a rendezvous with him by just minutes ... *Arrgggg*! Oh well. So even though I'm up to my ears in vocal elk, not only can't I get a shot, but so far I can't even get a peek. I'll have to be super careful not to spook these guys out of the Bowl area or my work will get a whole lot harder. And yours too, when you come next week. *Adios, monsieur.*

To Thomas Downing (third week of September): Sitting over Hillside Spring again last night, 6:45. The mountain had been uncharacteristically dead quiet all evening – not a bugle anywhere. In fact the singing's been tapering off for a few days now. The morning before, there was a bit of singing from the Thumb, up in the NW corner of the Bowl, just as we were getting there, prompting Alex to run a stalk. But the bugling stopped and what he found when he got close wasn't any elk but a big brown sow black bear with two yearling cubs (likely the same trio I saw back on opening morning and got some marginal photos of). As a city boy this was a first close bear encounter for Alex and later he acknowledged in his musical French-Swiss accent that the experience had been "*On*-believable!" But no more bugling all day and the same yesterday morning and evening. My odds didn't seem exactly high. Sometimes, for their own reasons, an entire mountainside of elk will clear out and not return for a week or more. Riches to rags. That was my concern, as it sure seemed to have happened.

So I'm sitting there about an hour before dark and it's getting cold so I'm drinking a cup of hot tea from my thermos and thinking all these gloomy thoughts, when suddenly I heard what I knew was an elk tripping down the ridge to my left from the Meadows, plowing right down through the brush (50 yards away or so), as seems to be the pattern this

Elkheart's 4x6 Gift bull (Alex Bugnon)

year, rather than using the game trail that runs right beside my blind (in fact, when I'm not around and a few times when I have been, it runs right *through* my blind). The wind had been shifty and could have switched at any moment, typical hunter's luck, making me nervous as a preacher in a whorehouse. As soon as I saw that it was a nice 6x6 I got ready for a shot … and that's when the bull stopped for a look around, just about on my level along the hillside but 30 yards or so away through scattered trees and brush. At one point, he looked right at me but failed to see, dressed as I was in a dark brown plaid shirt, camo "outback" (flop-brimmed) hat and face mask.

That was a tense few moments for me. But apparently reassured that he was alone, the bull came on down to the bench and walked right into the spring pool to drink. When his head went down I waited to see if it would pop right back up again, as so often happens when prey species are at water and feeling vulnerable to lurking predators like lions and me. But he kept drinking and I began a slow draw, reciting my silent mantra-in-motion: full draw, solid anchor, shoulders locked back, pick a spot, follow through … and let one fly and saw it hit mid-chest and instantly disappear into fur and flesh. Given the steep downward angle of the shot, maybe 35 degrees, almost like a tree stand, I knew it was good if not quite perfect and the arrow would exit low from the off-side chest, with any luck slicing the heart as well as both lungs.

So many things that could have gone wrong, as they have so often before, but this time didn't. Sometimes the magic works! At the shot, the bull raised his head and looked around, then turned and started *walking* away, not running! But he was already, instantly, behaving oddly "relaxed" and made it only 15 yards before collapsing. Two deep rattling breaths, then quiet. Another elk, dead in seconds and never out of my sight! (In fact, I was able to grab my camera, which I always keep at the ready by my side in case a bear or other nongame anima   comes in, and got a quick fuzzy pic of the bull walking away, a bare instant before he went down.)

The arrow, as it had appeared, in fact had entered mid-chest and exited the low chest on the off side, barely missing the heart while missing all ribs coming and going; amazing. He's a strange, lovely bull with six points on the left side and only four on the right. Yet both main beams are of equal size so that at a glance the antlers look balanced. I try hard not to look at antlers once I decide to take a shot, and as I approached him a few minutes later and got my first good look I thought, what the heck, he's a 4x4! When I got closer and saw that the other beam had six long tines I was almost disappointed, having lost bragging rights to "the world's biggest 4x4."

I was alone, as usual — Alex had gone somewhere way on up the mountain, and we planned to meet at the truck around dark. Working alone, I had the animal quartered and bagged in under two hours, mostly working by headlamp as darkness soon came on. It would have been much faster had it not been for an annoying equipment malfunction — a cute little folding alleged "bone saw" I had recently bought in town proved to be utterly worthless. I mean, it won't cut even a green aspen sapling or make even a scratch on elk bone! Not wanting to take the extra time in the dark to remove the lower legs at the "knees" with a knife, I opted to leave the legs on until Alex and I came back in the morning for the pack-out. Like a lot of hunters, I guess I'm yet to learn the difference at a glance between gadgets designed to appeal to the art-prone human eye, and those that actually work. We need John Deeres out here, not Porsches!

Otherwise, perfect is the word for this kill. Lucky is an even better word. I carried out the tenderloins and backstraps last night, as I always do when bears are around, which they always are around here — sure was dark out there! — and Alex and I got the rest, including the head (another skull mount) in two loads this morning. Doc Dave, bless his curmudgeonly old heart, volunteered to cut and wrap the meat so that I can keep hunting with Alex. That's a long day's work and really appreciated! Now it's Alex's turn to make meat. And when he leaves in a couple more days I still have a cow tag to try and fill with that lovely snaky Osage selfbow Clay Hayes gave me. Oh, happy days!

In the end, this experience makes me rethink the value of silent times out there, sometimes spanning days with no bugling or cow talk whatsoever. Maybe the bulls decide to call a truce and take a day off from singing once in a while so that they can rest and eat and drink. Beats me, but it's something to think about: Even when we don't see or hear them for days at a time, usually they're still out there, invisible forest spirits.

So once again, after weeks of daily hunting and tons of vocal excitement but no shot ops whatsoever, even on a cow, suddenly I'm sitting there one quiet evening and up walks a dandy bull. Killing from ambush like that, with everything nice and relaxed and almost too easy, can be anticlimactic compared to all the effort and excitement and challenge that went before. Yet it's all of a piece, eh?

What a *gift* was this unexpected bull!

And just in time: There's already snow on the highest peaks.

Be well,

Dave

(*Thomas Downing*)

About the Author

DAVID PETERSEN has been a passionate traditional bowhunter since the mid-1950s, and a bona fide "elkoholic" since 1980. Across those years he has also been a Marine Corps chopper pilot, a self-described beach bum, a student and college teacher, a hunting guide and professional conservationist, a magazine editor, homesteader and author. This is his tenth book dealing with "wildlife, wild places, and wild people with wild ideas," at least half of which have to do with the great outdoor loves of his life: elk and elk hunting.

In 2011 David Petersen was honored as Sportsman Conservationist of the Year by the Colorado Wildlife Federation. In 2012 CWC added to that honor with a Lifetime Achievement Award. In 2013, David received the Backcountry Hunters and Anglers Chairman's Award for outstanding service. Reading from that award announcement: "David Petersen is a hunter-conservationist who has been actively involved in BHA since the first year (2004) it was formed. ... David's many books and other writings related to hunting and conservation form the ethical foundation of BHA."

For the past 30 years and more David Petersen and his wife Caroline have lived in a self-built cabin high on the West Slope of the Colorado Rockies.